Strategic Management

SAGE COURSE COMPANIONS
KNOWLEDGE AND SKILLS for SUCCESS

Strategic Management
Chris Jeffs

Los Angeles • London • New Delhi • Singapore

First published 2008

SAGE Publications Ltd
1 Oliver's Yard
55 City Road
London EC1Y 1SP

SAGE Publications Inc.
2455 Teller Road
Thousand Oaks, California 91320

SAGE Publications India Pvt Ltd
B 1/I 1 Mohan Cooperative Industrial Area
Mathura Road
New Delhi 110 044

SAGE Publications Asia-Pacific Pte Ltd
33 Pekin Street #02-01
Far East Square
Singapore 048763

Library of Congress Control Number: 2007943039

British Library Cataloguing in Publication data

A catalogue record for this book is available from the British Library

ISBN 978-1-4129-4768-8
ISBN 978-1-4129-4769-5 (pbk)

Typeset by C&M Digitals (P) Ltd., Chennai, India
Printed in India by Replika Press Pvt. Ltd
Printed on paper from sustainable resources

contents

introduction to your course companion

Whether you are aware of it or not, the purchase of this book is the result of your strategic plan! Most likely, you have considered the subject of business strategy and having reviewed some textbooks and perhaps attended a lecture or two, you have decided that you may need some additional help. You have considered the options and have made a decision to acquire an additional resource. Having concluded that the investment is small, and the risk of wasting your money even smaller, you have rightly convinced yourself that this SAGE Course Companion will help you to achieve your goal. In strategic terms, you have undertaken a rational approach to the strategic management process; you have had concerns, evaluated what they are, considered the options and acquired a resource to help you to achieve your objective.

An additional influence on your decision to purchase this book is the use of your prior knowledge, learning and experience. You have bought books before; you know what you are studying; you know how much you can afford to spend; you might have some information about other textbooks that you will use and how this Course Companion complements these. This learning experience can add 'flesh' to the 'bones' of the evaluation which provided a supporting framework for your strategic decision. Combining research and experience will optimise the chance of success and this is the basis of strategic management.

This SAGE Course Companion will help you to understand this evaluation and decision-making process by providing a route map of key themes and authors to guide you through what, at first sight, may appear to be a daunting subject. It does not intend to replace your textbook, or indeed your lecture notes, but it does aim to give you a different perspective in a conveniently sized, easily readable format. It will also save you time searching through large strategy books in order to get at the core concepts!

> **Note**
>
> One of the great advantages of studying business strategy is the wealth of examples that are routinely discussed in newspapers and news reports. These provide an ideal opportunity to think about what you are studying and apply the theoretical concepts to the article. This means that when it comes to your examination, the availability of recent examples and the ability to extract the relevant information and make important connections will be second nature to you, and will help you to achieve the best marks.

How to use this book

Business strategy is such a broad subject that students often find it difficult to assimilate the key aspects of the study, especially with other subjects competing with their study time. The SAGE Course Companion has been designed with this in mind. It is a learning tool which will support your reflective study during your course and will also act as a revision guide towards the end of your undergraduate course. However, it is not intended as a short-cut to everything you need to know! You are strongly advised to use your textbooks and a wide range of other sources of material in order to gain a greater depth of understanding.

The textbooks referred to in this SAGE Course Companion include:

Coulter, M. (2008) *Strategic Management in Action*. 4th edn.
Johnson, G., Scholes, K. and Whittington, R. (2008) *Exploring Corporate Strategy*. 8th edn.
Lynch, R. (2006) *Corporate Strategy*. 4th edn.
Thompson, J.L. and Martin, F. (2005) *Strategic Management: Awareness, Analysis and Change*. 5th edn.

The SAGE Course Companion will help you to make important connections between otherwise seemingly disjointed subject areas. It provides examples of examination questions and a guide to the answers that will be expected for each, and also attempts to identify many of the common mistakes that students make in their use of strategic tools and theories. A significant portion of the guide also provides a link between your theoretical study and learning styles, with hints and tips which will not only help you in your business strategy studies and examinations, but will also provide a useful framework for other undergraduate modules.

Note

Business strategy is not a good subject to cram at the last minute. It is better to slowly absorb and build your knowledge during your course, using this Course Companion as a guide during this process.

The book is helpfully subdivided into three sections.

The first Part in the book will provide the background to the study of business strategy. An awareness of the historical development of a subject often helps to provide the basis for the teaching of it, as it provides a chronological series of developments and a broader context to your studies.

The second section provides the bulk of the academic material which you will come across during your studies. You will be assessed on the correct use of this material!

The third section focuses on the learning and assessment aspects of your study. It deals with different approaches to learning and will help you to make the most of your education. It covers a wide range of concepts, such as case study analysis, structuring assignments, referencing, critical thinking and getting the most from your sessions with your tutors.

All three sections contain common features which include:

- a summary of the most commonly taught tools, frameworks and theories
- reminders of the key themes to highlight in your examinations or assignments
- important links between topics, which you can use to demonstrate a broad understanding of the subject
- examples of 'real world' scenarios to put the theory into practice; these might also be useful to put in your answers
- example examination/assignment questions which will give you an insight into what may be required
- common errors and omissions that students make when being assessed
- key terms and definitions that are highlighted and listed in the glossary
- notes and tips that act as important reminders and clarifications on the subject
- 'Taking it further' sections that look at the subject in-depth or from a critical perspective. These can be useful to demonstrate to your tutor that you have a deeper knowledge of the subject
- links to chapters in commonly used textbooks to provide further reading and development of your understanding.

part one
strategy

1.1

thinking like a strategist

There is a debate about whether business strategy is a science or an art or, in other words, is it all research and planning or predominantly based on learning, experience and 'gut feel'? The historical development of the subject can add a valuable insight to both this debate and the way the subject is taught. Below is the briefest history of key developments in strategic management; it is certainly not a comprehensive list but it does illustrate some valuable points.

- **1900–1950:** The development of modern management theory starts with the scientific and administrative management models of Frederick Taylor and Henri Fayol. Their industrial experience emphasised the need for hierarchy in management, time and motion studies, close supervision and rewards based on performance. At this time, Max Weber characterised these models with a focus on documentation, rules and procedures or, in other words, bureaucracy. In America, Ford developed these concepts further with the emphasis on automated production, cost-cutting and quality standards.
- **1950–1970:** It was not until after the Second World War that the study of strategic management became a subject in its own right. The rapid development of world economies, particularly those of the USA and Japan, gave rise to large multinational organisations which required new ways of thinking. Formulated from his studies of successful Japanese companies, Edwards Deming introduced the concepts of *Total Quality Management* (TQM) which, for the next decade, was to revolutionise many western organisations. During this time, Igor Ansoff produced the growth development matrix, strategic gap analysis and many of the strategic terms we use today. Alfred Chandler introduced his seminal work linking strategy to structure; and Peter Selznick introduced the concept of matching internal resources with the external environment, culminating in a SWOT analysis. Peter Drucker introduced the world to management by objectives and team-based working. It was during these decades that the widely used concepts of environmental turbulence, environmental analysis, long-term planning, growth strategies and the range of theories which form the basis of prescriptive corporate strategy were developed.
- **1970–1980:** This decade sees the birth of market-focused organisations. Theodore Levitt and others argued that organisations should be customer-focused and should develop products that the customer wanted rather than

developing products and trying to persuade customers to buy them! The Boston Consulting Groups (BCG) portfolio matrix allowed for product analysis of the newly formed diversified organisations and strategic business units (SBUs). However, authors such as Kenichi Ohmae were also claiming that corporate strategy in the USA was too analytical and should be more flexible and intuitive, or more like creative art.

- **1980–1990:** In this decade, Michael Porter was perhaps the most influential writer on business strategy, contributing in particular to the area of sustainable competitive advantage, strategic groups and the important concept of the value chain. However, this decade was experiencing turbulent world economies, driven in part by increasing free market competition, major acquisitions, new digital technologies and ultimately the pressures of globalisation. Large corporations were now facing a challenging and dynamic business environment that required flexibility and accurate forecasting for strategic planning to be effective. Under these circumstances, authors such as Henry Mintzberg questioned the usefulness of long-term strategic planning and the theories of adaptive and emergent corporate strategy became more prominent.

- **1990–2000:** In order to keep place with dynamic environments and provide a sustainable competitive advantage, Peter Senge introduced the world to the concept of the learning organisation, in which he encouraged the gathering, analysis and sharing of knowledge. In this new world order, Jay Barney identified the importance of coordinating key resources and configuring them in an optimal manner. Also, the concepts of strategic intent and strategic capability were popularised by C.K. (Coimbatore Krishnarao) Prahalad and Gary Hamel and John Kay. They emphasised the importance not only of internal resources but also the management of distinctive capabilities and core competencies in order to generate a sustainable competitive advantage.

When reviewing the early development of strategic management, it is clear that an initial emphasis on scientific methods of management has led to a prescriptive or rational approach to the analysis of the environment, which was then used to plan for the long term. However, during the 1980s, such was the rapidly changing nature of the world's economies these concepts were proving to be outdated. More flexible approaches, which put more emphasis on internal capabilities and market demands rather than external influences, were required. This does not mean that current strategic management does not take note of the environmental situation. Clearly, this is still important. But the dynamic nature of the markets requires that any long-term planning must be adaptable in order to account for unforeseen events.

Note

While large organisations still attempt to plan for the long term, smaller companies are often limited to strategic planning over a shorter time period, perhaps only one year ahead with a three-year vision. These strategies will also be highly attuned to those of the financial backers.

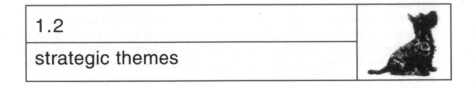

1.2

strategic themes

There are themes in business strategy that are common to all textbooks. These are:

- **The strategic analysis of the environment and the industry.** A good working knowledge of these tools will provide a detailed analysis of the external environment and industry, including any possible threats to or opportunities for the organisation.
- **The strategic analysis of the organisation.** An in-depth study of the resources, value chain and culture of the organisation can provide interesting insights into its inherent strengths or weaknesses.
- **An evaluation of markets and the competitive situation.** These theories are used to analyse the interface between the organisation and its markets and include market segmentation, strategic groups, and portfolio and competitive analysis. This information should be combined with the environmental analysis to provide a broad perspective.
- **Mechanisms of growing and developing the organisation.** These theories can be used to evaluate the organisation's growth options and include market development, product development or diversification. Growth can be by internal development or external development, for example by franchising, alliances or acquisitions.
- **Internationalisation and market entry strategies.** When entering a new international market, entry strategies such as exporting, licensing, mergers and acquisitions and foreign direct investment (FDI) will be considered. The impact of the forces of globalisation on the industry should also be evaluated, alongside the

alternative international organisational structures, in order to demonstrate appropriate control and coordination of the organisation.

- **Evaluation of strategic choices**. This is your chance to add value to your studies by showing an in-depth knowledge of your understanding of the environment, industry, markets and the organisation by identifying and summarising the key factors and interrelationships that you have discovered in your analysis. You may be asked to recommend a way forward for the organisation, so it is also your chance, for a short while, to be the Chief Executive! You will need to consider the suitability, feasibility and acceptability of each of the strategic options and make recommendations based on your findings.
- **Implementation of your strategy**. This is not as easy as you might think as it is all about ensuring a successful strategic implementation. When implementing your strategy, changes to the structure and control of the organisation are likely, and this will need to be supported by a range of change management tools. Stakeholder analysis may highlight groups of people who are for or against your strategy; you will also need to consider how you are going to win the dissenters over.
- **Other strategic issues** that the organisation leader should be aware of include innovation, creativity, technology and knowledge management, and corporate social responsibility. These will impact on any strategic decision that you propose, so you need to be looking to manage these to your organisation's advantage.

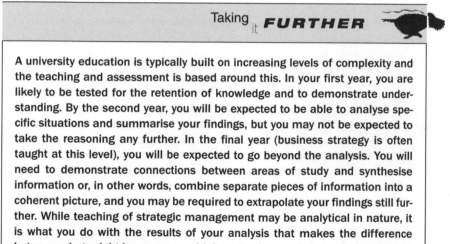

Taking it **FURTHER**

A university education is typically built on increasing levels of complexity and the teaching and assessment is based around this. In your first year, you are likely to be tested for the retention of knowledge and to demonstrate understanding. By the second year, you will be expected to be able to analyse specific situations and summarise your findings, but you may not be expected to take the reasoning any further. In the final year (business strategy is often taught at this level), you will be expected to go beyond the analysis. You will need to demonstrate connections between areas of study and synthesise information or, in other words, combine separate pieces of information into a coherent picture, and you may be required to extrapolate your findings still further. While teaching of strategic management may be analytical in nature, it is what you do with the results of your analysis that makes the difference between what might be a pass or a high grade. Successfully achieving this will also require an element of critical thinking, a subject that is discussed in Part Three of this SAGE Course Companion.

part two
core areas of the curriculum

2.1

what is strategy?

The term 'strategy' has been used for thousands of years and has typically been linked with military planning and tactics, but strategies can equally apply to organisations. One of the fundamental questions a business manager asks is 'What is the secret to being successful?' The answer is not self-evident; if it was, then anyone who studied *business strategy* could be successful! Nevertheless, all organisations need to plan ahead and adapt to external changes by adjusting their resources to best meet them.

Business strategy is the management of the organisation's resources and competences in order to match the aims of the organisation and the threats and opportunities in the environment.

The good news is that there is evidence to show that organisations which undertake strategic planning do tend to perform better than those organisations that don't. Regardless of the type of organisation, the strategies that they implement will be concerned with fulfilling the organisation's objectives and ensuring long-term survival.

Profit-orientated businesses are most likely to be concerned with growth, *competitive rivalry*, cost control and possibly shareholder value; their strategies will reflect this. Examples of strategies might include the automation of manufacturing processes, launching new products and undertaking *strategic alliances*. *Not-for-profit organisations* such as charities are most likely to be concerned with strategies that raise money in order to provide a service which fulfils a need and achieves the objectives of the organisation, such as advertising their purpose and growing their influence and membership.

Small-to-medium enterprises (SMEs) also have a vision and short-term strategies to help in getting there. However, their major goal is most likely to be focused on how to survive for the next 12 months and other 'small company' issues such as:

- cash flow and how not to run out of it
- getting known – the cost of advertising versus the increase in revenue
- location – where the best position to attract customers is versus the cost implications

- competition, in particular with larger organisations which have a much greater scale of economies and probably lower prices
- time, in which to do everything with limited resources
- expansion, recruitment and the cost of obtaining the necessary resources.

Their advantage over larger companies is that they are likely to be able to react quicker to market demands and can often offer a more personal service. Hence their strategies should emphasise these.

Strategic management is important to all organisations because it provides a structured process of analysis, using tools and frameworks to study the external and internal environment and provides a logical approach to strategic decision-making.

Strategic management is the process of identifying, evaluating and implementing strategies in order to meet the organisational objectives.

The strategic management process also provides a convenient means for business students to study markets, industries and organisations! However, organisational strategy is as much an art as a science. Once the *strategic analysis* has been completed, the strategic decision-making starts. While this is often influenced by the analysis and mathematical models, experience and intuition play a vital role in the final decision.

Strategy is an interdisciplinary subject so students and practitioners alike should make use of knowledge gained in other areas, such as finance, marketing, supply chain logistics and human resource management.

The strategic management process has been frequently described and schematically drawn in order to highlight the key stages. These diagrams usually vary in design and terminology but the underlying theme is the same. Key issues are identified through an external and internal analysis; strategic development and an evaluation of each potential strategy is completed before the process of implementation occurs. Figure 2.1 shows the strategic management process that will be followed in this Course Companion and it closely reflects those in the recommended core texts. Figure 2.1 also demonstrates commonality and influence between subjects with overlapping circles, the darker circles representing the major topic areas. The numbers reflect the sections where the subject is covered in detail, an example of an appropriate framework or tool is shown for most of the stages.

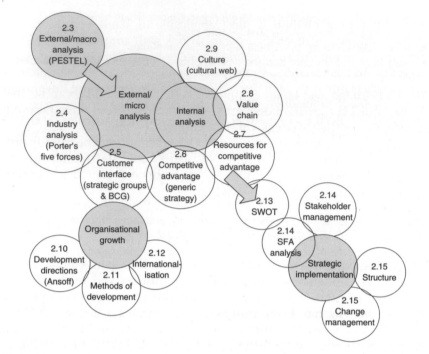

Figure 2.1   The strategic management process

Creating strategies

There are many theories, schools and approaches to strategy creation within organisations and this section will briefly differentiate between some of the most commonly taught ones.

> *Each approach to strategy creation uses different terminologies so you should try to identify the attractions and limitations of each theory, take the key themes and use them to your best advantage.*

Intended or *planned development*

Also called the *prescriptive*, positioning or design approach, it emphasises that strategic management is a rational process, analysing where the organisation is, where it wants to go and how it is going to get there. This formal planning method is most applicable in stable conditions and within complex or diversified organisations with control and coordination from the top down. Corporate strategy is predefined through three stages of strategic analysis, strategy development and strategy implementation (see Figure 2.1), each one actioned in a sequential and linear manner (*procedural rationality*). The development of the process has been heavily influenced by modern economic theory, in particular by that of Kenneth Andrews (1971), Igor Ansoff (1965) and Michael Porter (1985). This is the theory that most undergraduate business students study and is therefore the basis of this book. It may be popular because it is particularly relevant or because it was the earliest form of strategic management theory or possibly just because it is easy to deconstruct.

> A key differentiator of planned development is that the objective is defined in advance of strategic development.

Emergent strategic development

In the 1950s, several academics, in particular Herbert Simon (1960) and Charles Lindblom (1959), considered that corporate strategy was more experimental in nature and developed over time by adapting to changes as and when they are required (*logical incrementalism*). Because the final objective is unclear and strategies are implemented on an incremental and continuous basis, it has no long-term plan or process and is therefore unstructured in form. However, this approach does not completely ignore all the stages of linear strategic management. Strategic analysis is still important, but strategic development and implementation are inseparable and are based on experience, trial and error and adjustment.

Note

This approach may appear to be random and reactionary but many organisations undertake this form of strategic management and claim that in a rapidly changing environment long-term planning is of little use.

Authors in this area, such as James Quinn (1980) and Henry Mintzberg (1990), claim that strategic development is too complex for a prescriptive approach as it does not take into consideration the fallibility of the managers, the culture, politics or the experiential learning ability of the organisations.

However, the supporters of the prescriptive approach still emphasise the importance of long-term corporate planning – basing decisions on evidence rather than the 'gut-feel' of the emergent approach. They consider the involvement of key stakeholders in strategic decisions as being preferable to just 'muddling through'.

Note

In reality, both forms of strategic management occur to some extent. For example, planned long-term strategies may be modified by trial and error or influenced by experience as they are implemented.

In order to reduce the emphasis of a centralised or 'top-down' approach, organisations often use strategy workshops where a group of cross-functional managers or executives identify key issues and opportunities and debate how best to address them. The reassuring thing for the strategy student is that whoever is making the strategic decisions, they use many of the frameworks that you are studying!

Industrial organisation (I/O) or resource-based view (RBV)

When creating strategies with either model, the organisation will be influenced by both the external environment and its internal capabilities and resources. The industrial organisation approach first considers the external influences such as the profitability of the industry, its markets or the competitive situation, and adapts its internal resources accordingly.

The *resource-based view* will consider the unique resources and capabilities (including knowledge) of the organisation and its value chain and exploit these in order to generate a sustainable competitive advantage. The basis for this process is that the organisation builds on its strengths, which can lead to innovation and creativity in the market place.

Note

In reality, all organisations need to be continually aware of both the external environment and internal capabilities. At different times and under different circumstances, one or the other will be more important. However, long-term sustainable advantage is unlikely to be created by merely monitoring and following the external environment and leaders in the industry.

E–V–R congruence (environment–values–resources)

This means of strategic analysis provides a simple framework to evaluate the organisation's current needs and strategies. The concept of *congruence* is simply ensuring that each of the three key factors (environment, values and resources) are integrated into a singe coherent strategy, thus ensuring a good fit of all the essential components. The environment represents the key success factors (opportunities and threats); the *resources*, which include the organisation's competences and capabilities (the strengths and weaknesses), and the values that relate to the leadership and cultural influences of the organisation.

You might note the similarity here with the terms used in a SWOT analysis. Indeed, the SWOT analysis is useful in identifying the external and internal factors that should be considered in the E–V–R congruence framework. The evaluation of the closeness of fit between each of these SWOT aspects with the leadership values and culture of the organisation provides an insight as to the quality, appropriateness and likelihood of success when implementing the strategy.

Taking it *FURTHER*

It would be ideal if every organisational leader had time to strategically plan for the future, but in reality they often have to react to multiple and often unforeseen situations which they manage by applying their own preconceived ideas and expectations. In recognition of the fact that managers can only handle a limited number of options at any one time and bring their own biased perspective to every situation, the term '*bounded rationality*' has been coined. It implies that not every situation is optimally evaluated because humans are limited by their experience and capabilities. Under these circumstances and under the influence of other internal and external 'political' pressures, managers often compromise and settle for a mediocre solution rather than the optimal solution. Herbert Simon (1955) coined the word '*satisfice*' to describe this effect.

EXAMPLE QUESTIONS

The following are typical multiple-choice and short-answer questions which will test understanding of the most commonly used terms and models.

1 *Which of the following best describes the process of strategic management?*

   (a) *Strategic management is the process of determining and meeting the requirements of the stakeholder groups that are affected by the organisation's activities.*

   (b) *Strategic management is the process of identifying, evaluating and implementing strategies in order to meet the organisational objectives.*

   (c) *Strategic management is the annual planning process which determines the financial targets and budget allocations.*

   (d) *The strategic management process identifies organisational issues and provides a plan to addresses them.*

The answer is (b) as it contains the key themes of analysis, evaluation and implementation linked to the organisational objectives. The other answers are either too narrow in their description or inaccurate.

2 *List the stages of the prescriptive approach to strategic management, briefly explaining the purpose and aims of each stage.*

The material required to answer this question is substantially covered in this section.

Essay questions requiring a critical debate include:

3 *Critically debate the advantages and disadvantages of the planning perspective versus that of the emergent perspective. Your answer should be fully referenced and clearly explain the different approaches to strategy formation.*

4 *Is it desirable for an organisation to base its strategy on both fitting in with its environment and the development of unique capabilities or should it choose just one approach?*

The answers to these questions will be based mainly upon academic theory and could therefore be constructed as a literature review, discussing and debating from different academics' perspectives. As with any literature review, you (as the author) should remain unbiased and, unless specifically requested, you will not be expected to offer your own opinion. Some of the key authors have been identified in the preceding section.

An alternative type of question might be related to a particular organisation which you might be expected to analyse. For example:

5 *Using a well-known organisation, analyse whether the resource-based view or the industrial organisation perspective has been the predominant influence on the strategic development of the organisation.*

It is important when answering this question to link the academic theory with the strategic position at different stages of the organisation's development. You might find that drawing a timeline of key events and influences and identifying the strategic perspective of each provides a useful structure to your answer. Don't forget to summarise your thoughts in relation to the question at the end of your answer.

Textbook guide

COULTER: *Chapters 1 and 2*
JOHNSON, SCHOLES & WHITTINGTON: *Chapters 1 and 11*
LYNCH: *Chapters 1 and 2*
THOMPSON & MARTIN: *Chapters 1 and 2; Part 1, Supplement 1*

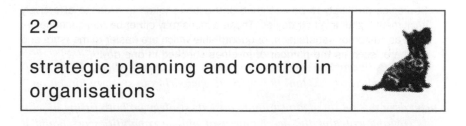

2.2

strategic planning and control in organisations

Levels of strategy

In the last thirty years, it has become the norm for organisations to develop a *mission statement* and these have often evolved into long texts which are elaborate, difficult to remember and vague. However, a good mission statement should succinctly communicate the broad vision, nature and underlying values of the organisation. Objectives may then be drawn from this and will be more specific, often time-limited and preferably measurable (closed objectives). For example, an objective might be to increase market share to 25% within two years or to improve customer satisfaction levels in some manner. However, there is little point in senior executives sitting in board rooms discussing the long-term objectives of the organisation unless strategies are put in place to ensure that they happen. In order to aid this process, there are different levels in organisations in which strategy is created and implemented; each of the three levels provides a different strategic perspective.

- *Corporate-level strategy.* Is predominantly concerned with the overall growth and development of multiple businesses within the organisation. It will be concerned with governance, geographic coverage, diversity of products and services, formal partnerships and acquisitions, allocation of resources and maximising *economies of scale* and *economies of* scope between business units and geographies. The corporate level strategies should aim to provide added value beyond mere management of the subsidiaries.
- *Business-level strategy.* At the strategic business unit (SBU) level, the aim is to gain competitive advantage in specific markets. Investment in research and development, and enhancing products and services on the basis of market research will be the emphasis here.
- *Operational strategies.* These are also known as functional strategies and tend to be based on shorter timescales. Operational strategies are concerned with how to deliver corporate and business unit strategies, especially with regards to the process of implementation and the allocation of resources. Strategies are likely to be designed and actions taken in order to effectively implement higher level strategies. These actions may either be non-quantifiable, such as customer satisfaction, or quantifiable which are easier to measure and compare, such as the number of invoices checked in one day.

Note

Each of these levels are not mutually exclusive but are linked. The corporate level strategies influence the business level strategies which in turn define implementation at the operating level. All strategies should be flexible and can be modified if necessary.

Strategic control

Strategic control systems are essential in order to check the progress of strategic implementation and should act as an early indicator of problems.

Strategic control is a form of corporate control which aims to manage the behaviour and efficiencies from a diverse range of business interests.

Strategic control is necessary as most executives are remote from the day-to-day activities of their organisations, and in any case there is usually too much specialised information to be able to quickly assimilate it. Typical control measurements might include:

- financial measures (costs, revenue, return on investment, profit, share price, etc.)
- customer satisfaction
- market growth and share
- quality measures, e.g. *Total Quality Management* (TQM).

Targets and budgets for the short, medium and long term are created at the top of the organisation and cascaded down; the resulting data is fed back up the organisation, to allow corrective action to be taken. Timely feedback of these factors, in relation to set targets, will provide both the manager and employee with a useful indicator of potential failure and success. For example, significant time and resources are often spent modifying internal quality processes, as poor process will lead to inaccuracies, re-work and increased costs.

> **Note**
>
> It is wrong to think that only the people at the bottom of the organisation's hierarchy are measured. All levels of an organisation will have targets and measures, it is just that each role and level will be tasked and measured differently.

Corporate-level missions and vision statements create a framework of objectives from which business units will create strategies; these translate into tasks and actions at the operational level. Take, for example, a company that has a vision or mission 'to create satisfied customers'. The strategic business unit may take a series of actions with the objective to improve the reliability of their products, for example, they may want to reduce the number of warranty returns. At an operational level, this might mean that new quality control checks are implemented and perhaps incoming raw materials will have to meet higher specifications. Each of these stages could be measured against considered targets and the resulting data is routed back up the company's management structure in order to provide feedback on progress of the new strategies.

Control systems may be categorised as:

- *Feed-forward* – anticipating problems (e.g. drug testing of employees)
- *Concurrent* – problems solved in real time (e.g. Total Quality Management (TQM))
- *Feed-back* – rectified after the event (e.g. sales revenue or customer survey).

Systems such as the balanced scorecard, Hoshin plans and traffic light charts are often used as a concurrent or feed-back form of control. A green light indicates over-target achievement, amber on-target and a red light under-target achievement. Individuals, including senior management, are allocated a series of targets according to their role. A quick look at the table of traffic light indicators highlight those targets which are being met and those which are in need of attention. The advantage of such systems is that complex target-setting and numerical measures are condensed into a simple visual comparison. The systems are highly adaptable to each level of *hierarchy* and can be adjusted according to changing strategy and the environment.

Note

The disadvantage of any form of measurement is that it does take time and it tends to focus attention and effort on meeting targets rather than on 'doing the job'. Also, if targets are inappropriately set, it can mean that other vital tasks are not being performed and that day-to-day cross-functional effectiveness, creativity and problem-solving may be stifled. For example, large organisations, in particular those in the public sector, tend to measure and monitor to such an extent (micro-manage) that this can detract from the day-to-day activities and true aims of the organisation. This has often been claimed in the case of the National Health Service and police forces, where form-filling and the meeting of targets detract from other essential services.

Corporate objectives and measures are often published in annual reports and it is not unusual to also be able to view the key measurements, if not the outcomes across multiple business units. For strategy students, these targets and objectives are a short-cut as they can provide an insight into the organisational strategy, if not the relative success of each corporate measure.

Organisational issues

There are a wide range of organisational concerns that strategists will have to contend with, many of which have only become apparent over the last two decades. Some of these factors are driven by trends in *globalisation*, with product and consumer needs becoming increasingly standardised, and also the dispersal of manufacturing to other countries in order to gain a cost advantage. These and other organisational developments are categorised and summarised in Figure 2.2.

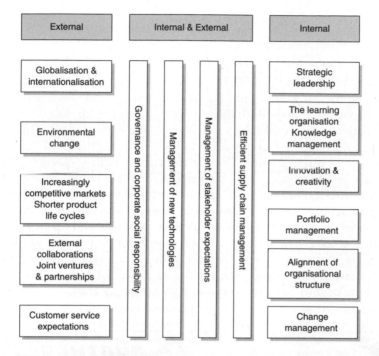

Figure 2.2   Organisational issues

Each of these factors will impact on all organisations to a greater or lesser extent and will need to be strategically managed. This highlights the important and complex role that modern organisational leaders have to undertake in order to steer an organisation to sustainable success. A leader therefore needs to fully understand the ramifications of such decisions and care needs to be taken when implementing a new strategy as it may impact on other areas of the organisation. A detailed discussion of each of the issues in Figure 2.2 is outside the scope this book. However, several key leadership issues are discussed in section 2.16 and many of the other strategic issues are included in the debate on strategic management and strategy implementation.

Strategic drift

Strategy development and implementation rarely happen as a continual process but may come in staged phases over a period of time. If these strategies lose sight of key external issues, then *strategic drift* may occur.

Strategic drift occurs when organisations do not adequately address the long-term strategic position of the organisation, which then results in underperformance.

There is a distasteful theory that if a frog is placed in water which is then heated, it will boil to death. If, however, it was dropped into a pan of boiling water, then it would jump out. It is hoped that no one has tried this experiment, but it does illustrate how change may not be noticed when an organisation is surrounded by a slowly changing environment. This could, for example, happen if an organisation is overly concerned with managing short-term or internal issues. Under these circumstances, changing legislation or a new technology may be introduced which could make products obsolete with too little time to counter the threat. Often the only recourse in such circumstances is to undertake strategic renewal, possibly with a new leader, as was the case of Stuart Rose at Marks and Spencer or Lou Gerstner at IBM. In more severe cases, it will not be possible to turn the organisation around, as was the case with former typewriter companies Smith Corona and Royal, which failed to make the transition to word-processing or into other markets and now no longer exist.

Taking it **FURTHER**

In the public sector, the state will play a significant part in controlling organisations. However, the degree of influence will depend on the extent of political intervention. Two extremes of thought in this area are represented by the terms *laissez-faire* and *dirigiste*. The laissez-faire model broadly follows a free market model, which encourages competition based on a profit motive and therefore requires little political involvement, examples include the UK and the USA. The dirigiste model encourages state ownership and financial support of the public sector and some key industries, which are often operating in a monopolistic environment. The dirigiste model is followed to a greater or lesser extent by countries such as France, Greece and Italy. In reality, the situation is rarely clear-cut and some countries will have a mix of nationalised and state-owned industries in the public and private domain, depending on the perceived importance in controlling and influencing each of them. Hence, when considering the public sector in a specific geography, the degree of market freedom in the public sector will need to be evaluated on a country-by-country basis. Look for links here with Porter's diamond, which is covered in the next section.

EXAMPLE QUESTIONS

Questions in this area will be related to your understanding of the strategic levels, control of the organisation, the range of leadership issues and how these relate to organisational strategy. Multiple-choice and short-answer questions might include:

1 *Which of the following best describes the term strategic drift?*

   (a) *Strategic drift is an emergent approach to strategy which provides a strategic solution when required.*
   (b) *Strategic drift occurs when organisations allow their products or services to become dated, which leads to a competitive disadvantage.*
   (c) *Strategic drift occurs when organisations do not adequately address the long-term strategic position of the organisation, which results in under-performance.*
   (d) *Strategic drift is where strategy implementation occurs too late to meet the need.*

The answer is (c). The other answers are either entirely wrong or too narrow in their description.

2 *Using an example of a well-known retailer, explain how the mission statement translates into objectives and tasks and how these might be communicated throughout the organisation. Identify the main elements that require control and how these would be measured.*

This question requires students to understand the connection between a mission statement and objectives and how they are translated into tasks throughout the organisation. Use examples of different objectives, for instance, increasing revenue through sales promotions or supply chain efficiency. To illustrate your points, use examples of the control mechanisms that might be used, for example, financial reports or balanced scorecard systems.

An essay-style question is also possible. An example follows:

3 *The organisational environment has been characterised as chaotic, complex, dynamic and turbulent – all increasing the level of uncertainty for managers. Discuss how changes in environmental characteristics might affect the approach taken to the management of strategic change throughout the organisation.*

You might start your answer with a brief discussion of the major influences that cause a rapidly changing and dynamic environment. Highlight the role of information and communication technologies in speeding up *product life cycles* and changing the competitive and consumer dynamics in many markets. Follow this with the use of examples of environmental changes and how organisations have adapted to them. An awareness of external scanning and avoidance of strategic drift will form the basis of your answer. Note that the question is also looking to determine the external impact *throughout* the organisation, so show how a changing environment will impact at each of the different strategic levels.

Textbook guide

COULTER: *Chapter 1*
JOHNSON, SCHOLES & WHITTINGTON: *Chapters 1, 5 and 12*
LYNCH: *Chapters 10, 12 and 17*
THOMPSON & MARTIN: *Chapters 2, 10 and 16*

EXTERNAL ANALYSIS

2.3	
analysis of the macro (far) environment	

Environmental scanning

It is vital that organisations are constantly aware of all the possible influences that may impact on their businesses or, in other words, the key drivers of change. The more dynamic and complex the environment, the more uncertainty there is and the more likely it is that change will occur. So, in an attempt to be proactive, organisations undertake *environmental scanning*.

Environmental scanning is the process of evaluating the external environment at the macro and micro level in order to identify organisational threats and opportunities.

Scanning should be a continual process to maximise the opportunity and benefit from early recognition of the change. This might be likened to a wild animal being constantly aware of its surroundings, by looking for predators (threats) and at the same time looking for food or a mate (opportunities). In the case of organisations, these influences may be externally or internally generated.

Many texts divide the external environment into the macro and micro environment (alternatively, you might use the terms *far* and *near environment*). We will first consider the *macro environment*.

The macro environment includes all those influences that will affect every firm in the same industry or sector and often organisations in other industries.

Macro environmental factors might include government regulation, technological and economic changes and other things that the industry often has no control over. For example, if a change in export law is being introduced, it belongs in the macro analysis as it is likely to affect the whole industry (and possibly other industries) and not just the specific organisation.

PESTEL

When scanning the macro environment, it is important to be thorough in considering all the potential influences so, as a reminder, frameworks have been developed to aid this process. Over the years, additional areas for scanning have been added so that there is now a range of mnemonics or acronyms to consider. Your tutors may have their favourites, but are unlikely to penalise you if you have completed an alternative and perhaps more thorough analysis. This book will refer to PESTEL. Others include:

1 STEP or PEST, which stands for Political, Economic, Social and Technological factors.

2 SLEPT, which stands for Social, Legal, Economic, Political and Technological factors.

3 STEEPLE, which stands for Social, Technological, Economic, Ecological, Political, Legal and Ethical factors.

4 PESTEL or PESTLE, which stands for Political, Economic, Social, Technological, Legal and Environmental factors.

Whichever acronym you use, ensure that your analysis highlights the most relevant factors. The best students will concentrate their analysis on these and focus less on the minor and least important influences on the industry.

You might sometimes find that some environmental changes could be considered in several categories, for example, changes in environmental legislation might appear as a political or legal or environmental factor. This doesn't really matter so long as you have identified and discussed the importance of it.

Some students get confused over the word 'environment'. When the word is used in conjunction with *environmental scanning* it is referring to *all external influences*. However, when the word is used as an influencing factor (e.g. in PESTEL), it refers to the changes to the natural environment or ecological influences, such as recycling or carbon emission policy.

The political environment will provide a range of potential issues with regard to future taxation policy, trade regulations, governmental stability, unemployment policy, etc. For example, the Royal Mail may lose its postal monopoly in the UK and, as a result of this threat, efforts are being made to reduce costs and increase automation in order to create a more competitive organisation.

When looking at the economic environment, you are predominantly considering capital cost and availability and consumer demand. An evaluation of a country's statistical data provides an insight into all manner of factors, such as inflation rates, consumer spending, unemployment levels, exchange rates, etc. These will be closely linked to political factors and will provide information relating to past and current trends, but they will also help to predict future trends. For example, a highly educated population which is also suffering from high unemployment may prove to be a great opportunity to open a new manufacturing plant.

Don't leave your analysis there. Evaluate the potential positive or negative influence (opportunity or threat) and the impact that it might have on the industry. For example, increasing unemployment might mean cheaper labour but it also might reduce consumer spending.

When considering socio-cultural influences, you should consider factors such as changes in birth rate, increasing leisure time, increasing numbers of skilled graduates, growth in the spending power of the youth market or the number of people above pensionable age. These will all impact on the demographics of a consumer base and may therefore affect customer segmentation and buying patterns. For example, there is an increasing trend in families where both parents work. This might mean that they have additional spending power but also that they might not have the time (or inclination) to do the grocery shopping and therefore choose to buy online. A retail business might consider making the most of this opportunity by offering an e-retail solution.

When you are looking for technological influences, it is worth remembering that these may not just relate to the technological changes and their impact on the products. They may also have a direct impact on the value chain by enhancing production techniques, or providing new forms of distribution or by improving communication and knowledge transfer, any of which may prove to be a source of competitive advantage.

Many students automatically quote the internet as a force for good. While the internet is of enormous benefit to many industries and most consumers, it can also provide a threat. For example, retail travel agents have had their traditional market overturned by the 'do-it-yourself' capability that the internet has provided to the customer. The introduction of voice over internet protocol (VoIP), which provides low cost telephony over the internet, has led to a major downturn in business for traditional telephone exchange providers such as Siemens.

Environmental issues are self-explanatory and may include laws on waste disposal, energy consumption, pollution monitoring, etc. Companies are increasingly aware and are proactively tackling these areas in order to be socially responsible or to save on energy and waste disposal costs. For example, in the European Union the impact of laws on corporations taking the responsibility for the disposal of their products at the end of their useful life has encouraged many companies to redesign their products with recyclable, non-toxic materials. Organisations are also watching the debate on the possible introduction of carbon credit trading with interest.

Legal factors may also appear under one of the other influences, such as political issues, and may include such things as employment law, health and safety, product safety, advertising regulations, product labelling, etc. Often a single law will impact on many industries, for example, the new EU-wide no-smoking laws have affected not just the tobacco industry but also the entertainment, leisure and outdoor furniture industries.

Remember that each time you have identified a significant trend, you should explain why the changing circumstance affects the industry, when the change will occur and what impact it might have. In effect, ask yourself 'so what does this mean for the industry?'

Porter's diamond

Due to the wide range of environmental influences, including those discussed in the PESTEL analysis, each country will often provide a different competitive environment. Four country-specific influences or factors have also been identified by Porter (1990) and are collectively known as Porter's diamond. These can provide a unique competitive advantage when they support a national industry, and include:

- the firm's strategy, structure and rivalry
- home demand conditions
- related and supporting industries
- factor conditions.

There are a number of ways in which the firm's strategy and rivalry will affect a national industry. For example, a family-run business may behave differently from that of a publicly quoted company and this may be reflected in the nature of the national industries. This is the case in Spain and Italy, where the national industries are often amalgamations of family-run businesses which, because they are not publicly owned, will be managed differently. In Germany, the management systems are predominantly hierarchical and process-driven, which has led to a high degree of technical engineering excellence.

Note

An intensely competitive environment can result in technological advances that may not be seen in other countries which are less competitive. This has resulted in many industry leaders claiming that they welcome competition as it benefits both the industry and consumer.

Home demand conditions can lead to enhanced product development in order to serve a demanding domestic market. For example, the French are enthusiastic wine drinkers and therefore require high-quality wines. In Germany, there is a demand for high-performance vehicles that can make use of the *autobahns* where there are no speed restrictions. This, in conjunction with intense rivalry, has led to the development of a high-performance car industry which includes such brands as BMW, Mercedes, Audi and Porsche.

Related and supporting industries are necessary in many industries in order to provide mutual benefit by integrating value chains or by supplying complementary products. Examples include companies that develop software which are based near to computer manufacturers, or pipes and oil rigs that are manufactured in Scottish deep water ports in order to support the North Sea oil industry.

The final element is the factor conditions which include:

- natural factors
- human factors
- knowledge factors
- capital resources.

These factor conditions are often based on natural features such as fertile land providing the basis of agriculture in France; or human factors such as a large immigrant population providing low-cost labour and therefore cheaper products; or the 'self-start' culture in the USA helping to shape national characteristics.

> *These factors may be influenced and later developed and supported by political regulation, technological development or socio-cultural changes. For example, in several countries (the UK and the USA in particular), there is an unresolved debate on the ethics of genetic engineering and cloning. Governments that implement less stringent regulations are most likely to promote knowledge leaders in this field.*

Governments may also influence the knowledge and capital factors by providing:

- subsidies to firms
- tax advantages
- educational policies that improve the skill level of workers
- enforcing standards to establish high technical and product standards, including environmental specifications.

> *Each of Porter's four factors will affect the other, for example, factor advantages will not lead to innovation unless there is sufficient domestic rivalry. All factors can be influenced and enhanced by government intervention.*

Porter (1990) argues that a lack of resources also helps countries to become competitive (he calls it a factor disadvantage) on the basis that having a surplus does not encourage efficiency but the lack of something stimulates creativity. For example, Japan is short on space, which has encouraged Japanese industries to develop *just-in-time* (JIT) inventory techniques in order to reduce the requirement for storage.

The use of Porter's diamond will provide a useful dimension to your PESTEL analysis by providing additional information with regard to a particular country or region. This may influence corporate decision-making, particularly when deciding upon international market expansion or overseas production.

Taking it **FURTHER**

It is reasonable to ask if it is worth undertaking an external analysis at all, as any information that you gain will already be out of date and should therefore not influence any new strategy. While there is some logic in this reasoning, it is also important to anticipate changes well in advance, so timing is important because if an organisation can adapt to changes before they are implemented, they may be turned to their competitive advantage. Anticipation can more formally be managed as scenario-planning, and considering of all the possible long-term alternatives. By having a range of views of how the future may look, strategists can start to see patterns and potential risks and can then model contingency plans around them. Organisations are increasingly managing their risks by estimating the probability of the scenario happening against the probable impact on the organisation if it did happen (*risk management*). While this can be a very inexact science, it does, if nothing else, provide some 'blue sky thinking' about the best and worst case scenarios within which the strategist can work.

EXAMPLE QUESTIONS

Multiple-choice questions might test your knowledge on the categorisation of the PESTEL acronym or your understanding of Porter's diamond. Here is an example:

1 *Which of the following is not a factor condition?*

(a) *Environmental factors.*
(b) *Human factors.*
(c) *Natural factors.*
(d) *Knowledge factors.*

The answer is (a) environmental factors. While climate may impact on the natural factors, the environmental factors belong in the PESTEL analysis.

Essays on the macro environment are likely to include case study papers which may either be provided to you or you might be expected to research your own material. Questions are most likely to ask you to analyse the macro environment and to conclude with how these may affect the industry. Note that you are unlikely to be awarded extra marks for discussing industry- or market-related factors if the question asks only for a macro analysis. Two typical questions follow:

2 *Determine the environmental influences on the world-wide tobacco industry. Identify how these might affect future strategies.*

3 *Identify what future changes are likely in the global consultancy business in the light of the factors at play in the macro environment.*

You will note that neither of these questions specifically asks for a PESTEL (or Porter's diamond) analysis. You are expected to identify that these are required and use them to frame your answer. Your tutors will not just be looking for a list of factors that may be important. They will be awarding the highest marks to those students who have thoroughly considered all aspects of the external environment and selected the most important for a detailed discussion. Don't feel that you have to find a range of influences for each letter. Rather, concentrate on the important factors; this might mean that some letters/factors are not discussed at all. When composing your answer, write down why it will affect the organisation in a positive or negative way and, in your summary, how the organisation might react to it. Try to surprise your tutors by making connections between events or different industries; it is always possible that they have not considered these themselves!

Textbook guide

COULTER: Chapter 3
JOHNSON, SCHOLES & WHITTINGTON: Chapters 2 and 8
LYNCH: Chapters 3 and 19
THOMPSON & MARTIN: Chapter 4

2.4

analysis of the industry

The *micro environment* is often classified as everything within the industry, or alternatively, the part of the business environment that the industry might have some influence over.

The micro environment is predominantly concerned with the competitive dynamics and markets of the industry or sector.

This includes:

- the industry itself (competitive situation, strategic groups)
- the customer interface (market segmentation and products)

Clearly, this is a large amount of information to analyse and is likely to take longer to do than the macro environment analysis. However, tools are provided which help to ensure that you consider all the important factors that might affect the organisation's competitive situation and future development.

Porter's five forces

To identify the competitive nature of the industry and therefore its potential profitability, Porter's five forces framework (Porter 1980, 2008) is often used.

If used at the strategic business unit level (in order to accurately compare similar segments), this framework will help determine the following:

1 Assess the attractiveness and profitability of the industry.

2 Help identify the possible sources of competition in the industry.

3 Identify possible threats to the stability of the industry.

4 Help in the development of future strategies.

The five forces model considers the interrelationship between the following forces:

1   Buyer power.

2   Supplier power.

3   Threat of new entrants to the industry.

4   Threat of substitutes.

5   The competitive rivalry.

These forces are often influenced by factors that have originated in the macro environment, for example, a technological change or enhancement to a product may destroy the industries' status quo. An example of this was in the traditional watch-making industry which was completely changed after the introduction of low-cost electronic watches. This affected both the manufacturing industry and the market that it served.

> *If you get confused as to who the suppliers and buyers are, imagine yourself being between the supplier and buyer. The suppliers will be providing goods or services to you, while the buyers (other companies or the consumer) will be buying from you.*

Each of the five forces is often influenced by the other forces. For example, buyer and supplier power may both impact on the company by the relative power they hold. If there are a large number of suppliers providing similar products or services, then there will be several alternatives and this puts more negotiating power in the hands of the buying company. However, if there are a limited number of suppliers or buyers, or their transaction is *asset specific*, they are likely to be able to demand a more attractive price from the company. If a merger or acquisition occurs between buyers or between suppliers, this will in turn negatively affect the profitability of the organisation due to reduced choice.

Students often presume that because an individual buyer can choose between competitive products, they have high power. This is usually not the case as only major buyers which purchase on a national or multinational scale, for example, buyers for retail chains, wield this sort of influence; individual consumers may have choice but their decision not to buy is unlikely to concern the bulk manufacturer. However, high cost/low volume and bespoke goods and services will result in individual buyers having more power.

A limited number of suppliers or buyers is one potential issue but if alternative suppliers or buyers are available, the costs of switching between them may still be high. This may be due to different standards being used, different training requirements or on the basis that if there has been a previous investment, it might look like a reversal of a decision (a failure of previous policy) if a purchase was to be made elsewhere. Sometimes an organisation just stays with its current suppliers or buyers, not because it thinks that they are necessarily the best solution but on the basis of 'better the devil you know'!

Sometimes students assume that if raw material prices, such as steel, increase, then the supplier power will also increase. There is, however, no link, as all the buyers are likely to be equally affected and the increased price of the goods is likely to be passed on to the buyer. The competitive dynamic is likely to remain unchanged.

If an organisation is considering entering the market (*threat of entry*), it is likely to increase competitiveness between the existing companies and will therefore tend to reduce prices and profitability for the whole industry. However, the industry may be unattractive due to one or more of the following *barriers to entry*:

- The high capital investment required.
- The need for economies of scale and therefore large volume sales.
- The difficulty of access to distribution channels.
- The requirement for specialist technology or skills.
- High customer loyalty to existing companies.
- Retaliation from the existing companies.
- High switching costs.

> *It is important to remember that the barriers may just delay entry and the relative importance of each barrier will differ from company to company.*

A substitute is an alternative product or service that replaces the customer's need or fulfils a similar function. For example, if you were considering the rail industry, a substitute would be the use of an alternative form of transport (e.g. car, bus or cycling) rather than using a rival train company. However, it is also important to think creatively as a substitute to travelling to work might include working from home and therefore not use any form of transport at all. This type of substitute is called an indirect substitute and might also be an alternative use of the buyer's money, such as buying a new kitchen instead of a holiday.

> *A common error when using the five forces model is that students consider substitute products as a similar competitive product (i.e. from the same market segment). In the case of Porter's five forces, this is not classed as a substitute. For example, a substitute for Pepsi is not Coca-Cola but an alternative means to quench your thirst, such as water.*

Competitive rivals are those organisations that compete in the same sector (product or service) and for the same potential customers.

The degree or extent of rivalry will depend on a number of factors:

- The number and relative size of the competitors.
- The degree of differentiation of the products.
- High *fixed costs.*
- The maturity of the business.
- The likelihood of a price war.
- Exit barriers.

High *exit barriers* will reduce the probability of a competitor withdrawing from the industry. For example, the industry may have heavily invested in R&D or its own specialised 'industry related' assets; it might have long-term agreements with trade unions or possibly a historical and therefore emotional attachment to a particular industry.

It is important to fully evaluate these forces in order to determine potential threats and opportunities and therefore future strategy. A thorough analysis will attempt to link the macro environmental analysis to the micro analysis. For example, if your macro analysis (e.g. PESTEL) identified that trade barriers were being reduced (e.g. China entering the World Trade Organisation), this might affect the five forces model by increasing the number of low-cost suppliers in the industry. This in turn might provide the opportunity for cheaper imports which could result in increased profits, or increased competition, lower prices and decreased profitability.

> *Just because there are a low number of competitors does not mean that it is not a competitive market. A consideration of the maturity of the market and the other factors listed above will give a more detailed appraisal of the competitive situation.*

In a competitive analysis, it is also important to evaluate how companies strategically build defences. For example, a company may decide that a particular supplier is so strategically important in providing a reliable source of high-quality components that it acquires the company. This strategy not only secures an important supply of components but removes a potential supplier to the competitors. This in turn may limit the number of remaining suppliers, increase component costs to the remainder of the industry (supplier power) and drive up competitors' prices (or lower their profitability).

Taking it *FURTHER*

As with many strategic models, the five forces model does have its limitations. For example, it is competitive by nature, it doesn't consider alliances and partnerships and the model will only alter after significant shifts in the competitive environment have occurred. Also, the model is focused on profitability rather than the customer requirements and it doesn't consider the wider issues of employment and social responsibility. However, these limitations accepted, this model does remain an excellent basis for industry evaluation and should be used in conjunction with Porter's other analytical tools, such as strategic group analysis.

EXAMPLE QUESTIONS

If you are asked a multiple-choice or short-answer question on Porter's five forces model, don't expect it to be easy. After all, your tutor is trying to test your understanding not just your memory! A multiple-choice question might look like this:

1 *Which of the following does not affect the bargaining power of suppliers?*

(a) *The number of potential suppliers.*
(b) *The uniqueness of the supplier's product or service.*
(c) *Buyer switching costs.*
(d) *The cost of raw materials.*

The answer is (d). The others will either impact on the competitiveness of the supplier or the desire of the buyer to move to another supplier. The cost of raw materials has no direct impact on the supplier/buyer relationship as it will affect all suppliers.

2 *What strategic factors must be considered in the situation where barriers to entry are low but where suppliers have high power?*

The above question is looking for an answer which first identifies that entering the market is easy (i.e. none of the barriers to entry exist), but where the suppliers have a high level of control. All the possible reasons as to why the suppliers have high power should be considered, such as a monopolistic market, high switching costs or restricted access to resources. However, don't leave your answer there. Try to think of ways to overcome the possible restrictions, for example, by reducing the switching costs or finding alternative resources.

For essays on this subject, you might find some subtle word substitutions in the questions, for example, the key word 'competitive' might be exchanged for 'profitability', or you might be asked to evaluate the 'industry attractiveness'. Each of these forms of question is still expecting the five forces model, either on its own or in addition to other frameworks. For example:

3 *Evaluate the competitive nature of the European perfume industry.*

This question requires you to evaluate the industry using Porter's five forces framework, but if you have additional market information you might also be expected to discuss market share, market segmentation, methods of differentiation, alliances and product portfolios. (See later sections).

A less specific essay question often links the macro environment and that of the micro environment. For example:

4 *What main trends are identifiable in the business environment in general and in the automobile market in particular and which might affect BMW's strategy?*

This question requires the analysis of the macro environment (PESTEL) and that of the industry with the five forces framework. It is important in your answer to distinguish between the two and not to mix the macro environment with that of the industry and markets. If you can identify links between factors, it will be rewarded. For example, new legislation and taxation regarding waste emissions is likely to affect the competitive nature of the whole industry, increase the likelihood of product substitution, and increase investment in R&D, technologically based alliances and future engine design. Don't forget to analyse the automobile market segments, consider BMW's core markets and who their sector competitors might be (see next section). Which of the external factors will impact on the design and changing market of the automobile? What are BMW doing to anticipate the changes? For example, you might want to mention the addition of the Mini and other new small models to the BMW portfolio and discuss the reasoning behind the changing strategy.

Textbook guide

COULTER: *Chapter 3*

JOHNSON, SCHOLES & WHITTINGTON: *Chapter 2*

LYNCH: *Chapter 3*

THOMPSON & MARTIN: *Chapter 4*

2.5

analysis of the customer interface (markets and products)

Strategic groups and competitive analysis

Before analysing markets and products, it is important to distinguish between an *industry* and a *market*.

An industry is a group of companies that provide products or services that are similar.

The market is defined by the consumer or customer requirements, which in turn may be segmented by such things as geography, age, gender, religion, income, loyalty, etc.

Due to the complex nature of large organisations, they commonly belong to a number of industries and to even more *market segments*. A group of companies competing in the same industry (with similar products or services), with similar strategies and for the same customers, would be classified in the same *strategic group*.

If you are distinguishing between and comparing (benchmarking) organisations, it is important that you are comparing the same strategic group, otherwise your information will not be accurate. Organisations within the same strategic group directly compete with each other for the same *customer segmentation* or demographic. For example, if you were to compare PC retailers, high street PC retailers would all be in the same strategic group but internet retailers (e.g. Dell) may be in a different strategic group. However, if a high street retailer also sold directly through the internet, it would be in the same strategic group as Dell for that market segment.

It is also important to remember that due to technological convergence, and merger and acquisition activity, strategic groups regularly change. Technological convergence can be easily identified in the media and mobile communication industries. Service industries such as the airline industry can demonstrate how alliances blur strategic group boundaries as they now also offer car hire and hotel reservation services.

Knowing the strategic groups allows you to:

- focus on the key competitors
- identify opportunities in other strategic groups
- identify possible threats within each strategic group
- identify new markets in order to create a new strategic group
- identify possible synergies for potential merger, alliance or acquisition activities.

When comparing companies (or more likely strategic business units) within a strategic group, a table may be drawn up of the relative strengths and weaknesses of each company and product (or service) offering. A comparison is likely to include all the components of a micro analysis with resources, competences, supply chain efficiency and product differentiators also being considered. This will provide the basis for the development of strategies to enhance an organisation's competitive advantage.

When undertaking a strategic group analysis, analyse the main competitors first. If a company can successfully compete against these, the others should be less of a risk. Also concentrate on the main differentiators rather than listing every feature of each company; this will save you time and make your report more readable. Look for signs like companies selling 'at cost', gaining control of the distribution channels or making it difficult to switch to other companies. If the company is the market leader, it may be implementing these defensive strategies in addition to maintaining its product or service advantage.

When comparing market segments, make a judgement as to whether the company is a large fish in a small pond or a small fish in a large pond. It will provide an indicator of future potential growth and market share.

Product development and portfolio management – BCG matrix

When comparing the *product portfolio* of different organisations, a number of tools may be used.

A product portfolio is a range of products provided by the same company for different market segments.

The Boston Consulting Group growth-share matrix (more commonly known as the BCG matrix or the Boston Box) is a useful tool that may be used to display and compare products by market share and growth. The four quadrants include:

1 Star (high market share and high growth).

2 Question mark or problem child (low market share and high growth).

3 Cash cow (high market share and low growth).

4 Dogs (low market share and low growth).

Providing you have the relevant information, you can compare products within a single portfolio or superimpose the products of one company over that of another to act as a visual comparison.

Don't forget that the stage in the product's life cycle is likely to have a direct bearing upon its categorisation. You are unlikely, for example, to find a mature product nearing the end of its life as a star; it is more likely to be a cash cow or dog.

An organisation will usually prefer that its portfolio provides a varied range of products in order to capture as many market segments as possible. But they also require a succession of new and potentially profitable products. If a competitor in a strategic group had a number of new products that were rapidly gaining market share (stars) while another organisation only had low growth and declining products (dogs or cash cow) with no stars or question marks, a strategic threat (and opportunity) presents itself.

The development of new products will often be funded with the profits gained from a cash cow product (which requires relatively little expenditure). For example, most pharmaceutical companies struggle to maintain their vast research and development budgets and are hoping to develop a highly successful blockbuster drug or cash cow to fund future R&D.

In many industries, the expiry of a patent or the realisation that a patent does not cover a particular geography is an opportunity for competitors to develop similar technologies and products. The impact on the organisation can be so sudden that almost overnight the growth potential and market share position can change due to the entrance of a direct competitor. Returning to our previous example, successful drugs can be copied and manufactured in other parts of the world and sold in regions where there are no patents or where patents have expired. These low-cost equivalents are called generic pharmaceuticals and emphasise the importance of making a return on the R&D investment prior to patent expiry. Patenting is a double-edged sword: it provides a form of protection from copying (so long as the company is willing to defend it in the courts), but it also publicly details the advances made and future market opportunities. As an observant student, you may be able to identify these.

You may have noticed that it is often not a simple matter to complete (the precise market segment information may not be available for all competitors), or even evaluate a BCG matrix. For example, if an organisation has a high growth and high market share, a 'star' in its portfolio, it is not always good news. It might mean that it is maintained in that quadrant by high marketing expenditure, or possibly with a low price in order to 'buy the market share', which could be affecting the organisation's profitability.

Note

During the initial stages of development in a small organisation, growth and market recognition may be more important than high profits. Conversely, a large organisation may be satisfied with their market share and be looking to maximise their profit from it.

A low growth product may sometimes be beneficial to the organisation as the product may still be profitable and may also complement other products in the portfolio by providing product, resources or skills which are beneficial elsewhere. A media company, for example, might have a low growth and low market share (dog) film studio. However, this studio may also provide valuable and unique video input to other products in the portfolio and therefore might enhance the organisation's skills, flexibility and competitiveness in other ways.

> **Note**
>
> Note that the BCG matrix does not quantify risk and therefore is not useful for proposing future strategies. For example, even if a product is growing rapidly, it might be in a politically unstable geography where there is a risk of sudden failure. Under these circumstances, an important link to your macro environmental analysis could be made.

A thorough study of a BCG matrix might lead you to consider that the organisation might follow one or more of these strategies:

1   Build market share, for example, by investing in a question mark with the intention of turning it into a star.

2   Hold investment at a sufficient level which is enough to keep all the products in their current position.

3   Harvest by reducing the investment and therefore maximise the short-term cash flow and profits.

4   Divest products by selling or axing them. This might provide more finance to invest, for example, in question mark products. It might also allow the company to focus on an alternative portfolio of related products.

5   Research and develop new products to replace those that are coming to the end of their life cycle or are unlikely to be successful.

Taking it **FURTHER**

The BCG matrix does have a number of limitations, for example, the definition of market share and growth is a difficult one to qualify. A 2% growth rate where the market is otherwise in decline or in the off-season may be respectable; in other markets, more than 10% might be expected. Likewise, in a large, highly competitive, rapidly growing market, a relative market share of 2% may be considered good, particularly if the organisation in question is small in scale and perhaps lacking in resources. In particular, the definition of market segment is very subjective as a comparison of identical market segments is difficult; an organisation may have a large relative market share but be situated in a very small niche. Due to these limitations, other models, such as the McKinsey directional policy matrix, have been developed and work by comparing the industry attractiveness and the competitive position of the organisation.

EXAMPLE QUESTIONS

A typical multiple-choice question on the topic of the customer interface might include:

1 *Which of the following is an example of a strategic group?*

   (a) Airlines.
   (b) Quarried rock supplier.
   (c) Supermarkets.
   (d) Surfboard manufacturer.

The answer is (a) Airlines. The industry is not a single business unit as it contains multiple businesses and markets segments such as low-cost carriers, chartered flights, etc. The other answers are specific to single markets.

It is unlikely that you will be expected to undertake an essay or examination and only discuss strategic groups or the BCG matrix. It is more likely that these may be a part of a larger question, possibly relating to the competitive nature or marketing strategy of the organisation. The following are examples of short-answer and essay questions.

2 *Using examples, show why it is important to compare similar market segments.*

The emphasis of your answer should be based on the previously listed benefits of identifying strategic groups. If you can provide examples for each of these, it will gain you additional marks. You might also pick up a bonus by using examples to show why strategic groups might change.

A broader essay-style question might alternatively be asked:

3 *Using the BGC matrix, critically evaluate the product portfolio of Unilever, explaining the reasoning behind your analysis.*

This question requires detailed analysis of financial revenues of each product line and the relative market shares; if the data is not complete, you may have to make assumptions. Ask your tutors if they will permit this. If they do, make sure that you highlight why the assumption has been made and the reasoning behind it. Once you have completed your analysis, try to go beyond the BCG matrix and look for synergies between products, for example, in manufacture or possibly in distribution.

2.6
competitive advantage

Generic strategy and the strategy clock

Competitive advantage is a significant advantage over competitors which is achieved by offering the customer greater benefit through a lower price or added value.

There are a number of competitive strategy models which help to determine *competitive advantage*, and these include Porter's generic strategy (1985), Mintzberg and Quinn's generic strategy (1992) Miles and Snow's (1978) adaptive (competitive) strategies and Faulkner and Bowman's (1995) strategy clock. According to Porter's generic theory, competitive advantage is achieved through one of three strategies. They are called 'generic' as they can be applied to all product and service industries, both large and small. These strategies are:

- cost leadership
- differentiating the product
- combining either of the above with a focused or niche strategy.

The key features of the generic strategy model are that if an organisation can differentiate a product or service, then it can create additional value and benefit to the consumer and may then demand a premium price. Depending on the industry and market, *differentiation* may be based on one or more of the following:

1 Speed.

2 Reliability.

3 Service and customer relationships.

4 Design.

5 Technology and/or features.

6 Brand image.

Differentiation may be in a niche or narrow market, for example, a small geography or a particular product or customer segment, or it may be applied to a wider market (broad segment). For example, Bang & Olufsen demonstrate differentiation in a niche market with their technologically advanced, uniquely designed and premium priced audio-visual products.

> *Being in a niche market also benefits the company because it has a detailed knowledge of the segment and the associated brand encourages customer loyalty.*

An organisation that follows a differentiation leadership strategy is likely to exhibit one or more of the following key indicators or traits:

- a relatively narrow range of products
- an emphasis on marketing and branding
- creative design and packaging
- high expenditure on R&D
- a reputation for quality
- expensive headquarters and outlets.

If an organisation aims to be a cost leader, then it is focusing on efficiencies that are often achieved through economies of scale. Larger organisations are better positioned to do this and you can identify cost leaders by their emphasis on:

- a standardised and limited range of products
- tight cost control
- quality and performance targets

- close coordination between value chain functions, for example, with just-in-time (JIT) manufacturing and electronic point-of-sale systems (EPOS)
- simple-to-manufacture (automated) products
- low-cost distribution systems
- a short value chain (cutting out the 'middleman').

If you find a company that competes on the basis of cost leadership, it is a good opportunity to investigate its value chain to find out where its strengths lie.

Understandably, most companies aim to be efficient regardless of any other competitive strategy they choose to employ, but companies such as Bic (which make millions of simple, standardised pens, lighters and shavers) and EasyJet have developed this as their core strategy.

A common mistake is to confuse cost leadership with the price of the product. Cost leadership is independent of price. An efficient 'cost leader' organisation can be profitable at a high or low price. The profitability of a company following a cost leader strategy is higher than those not following a cost leadership strategy because their costs are lower. Also, note that a low-priced product is not always a guarantee that the company is following a cost leadership strategy; it may be looking for market share or to clear stock.

You will find that in many mature markets there are a number of companies competing with standardised products and a low-cost strategy. However, there may still be room for a differentiated focus strategy if a niche market can be found.

Don't assume that not-for-profit (NFP) organisations do not need to compete. Typically, they are competing for resources, customers, volunteers, members, donations, etc. Not only do they have to be highly cost-efficient due to the lack of resources, but they will also need to differentiate their service from other organisations.

Porter's generic strategy does not provide the option of a *hybrid strategy*. Indeed, it urges against 'being stuck in the middle' or, if you prefer, 'having no clearly defined strategy'. In this position, the products may not be cheap to produce and are not sufficiently differentiated and therefore the organisation is unlikely to be successful. However, unlike Porter's (1985) model, Faulkner and Bowman's (1995) and D'Aveni's (1995) models provide other competitive possibilities, which together might be classified as a strategy clock. The strategy clock uses differentiation and focused differentiation in a similar manner to that of the generic strategy model, however it also provides options such as competing on price and a hybrid or 'dual strategy' which provide additional flexibility.

Companies such as Benetton, Toyota or Ikea are examples of companies that compete using a hybrid strategy. By following a cost leadership strategy, they are able to maintain a healthy profit and provide a competitive price but they also maintain a differentiation strategy by providing a high product or service quality.

Price is of course a major contributor in most models of buyer behaviour. If a consumer is buying a product or service, then the price must reflect the expected benefit. The low price or no-frills strategy therefore might attract buyers with limited funds or perhaps those which require only occasional use. No-frills examples include a basic car wash service (no wax or polish) or an economy brand of a basic food like flour or sugar; as there is little perceived difference between these products, price becomes the major differentiator and therefore a competitive advantage.

> **Note**
>
> The strategy clock also provides alternatives of high price and little perceived benefit. However, unless the organisation is acting in a monopoly situation or in some form of protected market, such as a cartel, these are likely to fail.

Competing by price alone is also often exploited by new entrants into the market, but might only be sustainable for a short period of time unless the profit margin can be supported by a low-cost base. Price is also a key differentiator in many service organisations, such as cleaning companies, where a basic service is provided for a low price. However, if managed well, a low-priced product or service can attract loyal customers and, with a positive reputation, might enable the company to increase its price and differentiate by other means. A good example of this is the automobile manufacturer Skoda, which originally entered western markets as a low-priced unknown and has carefully managed its reputation so that it can now charge higher prices and differentiate itself in other ways.

> **Note**
>
> The danger of competing by price alone is that a company can quickly obtain a reputation for being 'cheap and cheerful' and might only be a buyer's choice by default, if they cannot afford the other higher priced options.

When analysing the competitive strategy of the industry, you could use either of these competitive frameworks as the tool for your analysis, but don't forget to compare like with like within the same strategic group and market segment. This can be complex but any other alternative will lead to an inaccurate and misleading analysis.

Building a competitive advantage through cooperation – four links model

An alternative means of gaining a competitive advantage is by cooperating with others through either informal agreements or contractually binding frameworks. This may enhance the organisation by sharing technologies or resources, improving supply efficiency or by enhancing the product. Because of this co-operation, they should also be considered when analysing the competitive nature of the industry.

> *Don't automatically assume that these links are always beneficial (a strength). Occasionally links may be time- and resource-hungry and the benefits may be minimal.*

Richard Lynch (2006) has classified four alternatives or links which include:

1 Informal cooperative links and networks (e.g. industry bodies which may improve standardisation or mutual support through a system such as Japanese keiretsu).

2 Formal cooperative links (e.g. alliances or joint ventures, often between suppliers, distributors and those offering skills or technology advantages).

3 Complementors (usually from different industries, e.g. MP3 player hardware and download software, or cameras and photo printers).

4 Government links and networks (e.g. as a supplier to government or by influencing policy).

Your macro environmental and industry analysis may show potential advantages of links but beware as they are often temporary in nature. The important message here is that when you are doing your external analysis you should be looking for both linking opportunities and threats from existing links.

Taking it *FURTHER*

Some students argue that branded clothing might fit into the hybrid category of high value product with no apparent benefit over the lower priced alternatives. However, the perceived benefit to the customer is the 'feel good' factor when wearing the product; the recent fashion of having the label or brand names on the outside of the product supports this claim. Consumers are prepared to pay more for the image that it projects. Hence these products fit in the focus differentiation category and will only be doomed to fail if the 'feel good image' disappears. This is of course why leading brands work so hard to maintain the status of their brands by protecting the market from cheap imitations.

EXAMPLE QUESTIONS

A typical multiple-choice question on competitive strategies might look like this:

1 *Which of the following is destined for failure according to the strategy clock?*

   (a) *High price/high perceived value.*
   (b) *High perceived value/low price.*
   (c) *Low perceived value/high price.*
   (d) *Low price.*

The answer is (c), low perceived value/high price, as the customer would not see any justification in paying more for a lesser product. The other alternatives provide acceptable purchasing criteria.

Questions relating to competitive strategy are often broader in scope and may include the use of other models, such as the BCG matrix or strategic group analysis. However, specific questions may be asked and might include questions along the lines of:

2 *Using examples, describe the relative advantages and disadvantages of Porter's generic strategy model with that of Bowman's strategy clock.*

This question is clearly theoretically based and requires a good functional understanding of the two models and some examples to illustrate your answer. The key differences between the models have been highlighted in the previous section and include, most importantly, the inability of Porter's model to use hybrid strategies or price as a differentiator.

3 *Critically evaluate the sources of Ford's competitive advantage throughout its history.*

This question is broad and the answer will benefit from being logically structured, preferably on a timeline. You might find examples of differentiation by technological advances or manufacturing and process enhancements that have been following cost leadership strategies. However, also look beyond the obvious and identify strategies that have been particularly successful in certain markets, possibly due to price competitiveness (a hybrid strategy?) or perhaps due to cooperative alliances or acquisitions.

4 *Using examples from the public and private sectors, explain why cooperation is sometimes better than competition.*

This question is not specific to any industry or organisation and so your answer is most likely to be based around the four links model with contemporary examples for each link. However, don't forget the basis of the question – a discussion of the disadvantages of competition is also required.

Textbook guide

COULTER: *Chapter 6*
JOHNSON, SCHOLES & WHITTINGTON: *Chapter 6*
LYNCH: *Chapters 3 and 13 (especially for cooperative links)*
THOMPSON & MARTIN: *Chapter 6*

INTERNAL ANALYSIS

2.7	
resource analysis	

An internal analysis provides a valuable insight into an organisation's resources which may result in strategies that build on an organisation's strengths, minimise weakness and identify capabilities that could result in a competitive advantage.

Strategic capabilities are the resources and competences of an organisation that enable it to successfully compete.

Strategic capabilities are created by applying the relevant resources at the right time and with optimal efficiency in order to allow an organisation to develop a sustainable competitive advantage. In order to make judgements on the skills and resources that an organisation has, it is important to undertake a resource analysis. Resources can be ranked in importance by categorising them as either *threshold* or *unique resources*.

Threshold resources are those resources that are required as a minimum in order to compete in a market.

Unique resources are those resources that are difficult to obtain and provide a clear opportunity for competitive advantage.

In order to evaluate the internal effectiveness of the organisation, an *audit* of the internal resources should first be made. When undertaking a resource audit, you should consider all the functional aspects of the organisation (e.g. marketing, operations, finance, human resources, R&D, information management, etc.). Types of resource include the following:

- **Financial.** Cash reserves, investments, holdings, shares, debts, etc.
- **Physical.** Buildings, machinery, raw materials, stock, etc.
- **Human.** Skills, knowledge, experience, diversity, competences, etc.
- **Structural and cultural.** Reporting processes, working relationships, etc.

Other terms that you will hear are:

- *Tangible resources*, which might include any quantifiable physical assets.
- *Intangible resources*, which might include patents, databases, reputation, brands, etc.

> *Remember that resources are not just absent or present and in the right quantities. It is important to consider if they are being managed and used effectively.*

The ultimate purpose of a resource audit is to identify one or more of the following factors:

- **Cost saving efficiencies**. Under-utilised resources may be identified and rationalised (e.g. spare capacity on a product line, reduction of purchasing costs and improvement in economies of scale).
- **Investment opportunities**. Areas that would benefit from additional investment can be targeted (e.g. IT systems to improve coordination of delivery).
- **Synergies**. Between different business units or departments providing an opportunity for resource or knowledge sharing (e.g. sharing automation technology between different factories).
- **Key capabilities**. These may be identified so that they can be utilised elsewhere (e.g. software development skills).

Benchmarking

Identifying, quantifying and tabulating these resources is an important first stage but analysis and comparison (*benchmarking*) should then follow. Benchmarking allows for a comparative analysis on a historical or competitive basis.

- **How have the resources changed over time?** For example, the number of employees may have been reduced due to new working patterns or increased automation.
- **How does the organisation compare against the rest of the industry and its direct competitors?** For example, in the case of a courier company, speed, reliability and geographic range are key indicators of performance which can easily be measured.

From the organisation's perspective, it can provide valuable information on how much they can improve their own processes to match that of the market leader. It can also reduce complacency and create new objectives. Organisations can also benchmark against other industries which may provide insights into performance improvements. For example, Formula 1 pit-stop teams were studied to aid the development of new critical care techniques used in operating theatres.

Strategic capability – VRIO

Once identified, the key strategic resource or capability may be further evaluated for its usefulness to the rest of the organisation. Jay Barney (2002) developed a series of questions which, when used as part of the VRIO framework, helps to determine the presence of competitive resources:

- Is it **V**aluable? Is the organisation able to neutralise a threat or create an opportunity?
- Is it **R**are? This could be long-term experience or a unique external relationship.
- Is it easy to copy? It may be too complex to **I**mitate.
- What is the potential for it to be used by the rest of the **O**rganisation?

Core competence

If the strategic capability meets all the above criteria, it is most likely to be a core competence. The concept of *core competence* was most notably developed by Gary Hamel and C.K. Prahalad (1990).

Core competences are a complex mix of skills and resources that provide a distinctive competitive advantage. They can be successfully applied to multiple areas within the business but are difficult for competitors to imitate.

Core competences may not be immediately obvious, so in addition to the VRIO evaluation there are three further tests to determine them:

1 A core competence must add value or provide competitive advantage to the products or services.

2 Core competences should be difficult for competitors to copy, hence they are likely to be unique.

3 Core competences provide potential access to a variety of markets – by assisting the development and adding value to multiple products or services.

The core competence of Honda, for example, might be its research institute, which, over the past sixty years, has produced many developments that have been utilised in innovative engine products in markets as diverse as motorcycles, generators, lawn-mowers and, most recently, fuel cells for cars. Pilkington glass has a core competence, developed over many years, that has led to a process that allows large sheets of glass to be made relatively quickly and to very high standards. This process and technology has led to the development of related manufacturing processes in other areas of the company and a licensing opportunity for other companies.

Note

Some students struggle to find a core competence in an organisation and may wrongly end up with the identification of a single skill or product as a core competence. But remember that smaller organisations which have limited technology or experience are unlikely to have developed a core competence. Even in large organisations, core competences are rarely obvious and might only surface once a detailed resource and capabilities analysis has been performed. Those organisations that have no identifiable core competences can often compete perfectly well by relying on their strategic capabilities.

You might have noticed that there is a great deal of similarity in the terms *'core competences'*, *'distinctive capabilities'*, *'strategic capabilities'*, etc., which means that they are often used interchangeably. The important thing is to identify what adds value and provides strategic benefit to the organisation – the term you use to describe this attribute is less important. Don't forget that a key capability need not be technology or market related but might also be a manufacturing process, the geographical coverage, a key alliance or even the culture of the organisation.

Taking it *FURTHER*

Many industries survive without having any clearly identifiable competitive advantage let alone core competences. This is most likely in organisations which do not need to compete, such as public sector service industries or those industries that produce commodity products such as oil and flour. Under these circumstances, products or services are sold predominantly on price but there is still scope to differentiate their products by branding or by adding complementary or enhanced services. Clearly, profitability can also be improved by following a cost leadership strategy.

EXAMPLE QUESTIONS

A multiple-choice question on this subject might be similar to the following:

1 *Which of the following best describes the term 'core competence'?*

   (a) *Core competences are the minimal capabilities in the strategic group that are required to obtain competitive advantage.*
   (b) *Core competences are the key resources that have been internally developed to support an organisation's strategic capability.*
   (c) *Core competences are complex capabilities that are central to the organisation's strategic capability.*
   (d) *Core competences are a complex mix of skills and resources that are difficult to copy and provide a distinctive competitive advantage across multiple areas of the business.*

The answer is (d). It is the most appropriate description of a core competence, the others being too vague and missing the key point of being a mix of specialist resources and skills which are difficult to imitate, and can be applied to multiple markets.

Essay questions that relate to resource analysis are most likely to be on the wider theme of internal analysis and strategy. You will be expected to use a range of frameworks, such as the value chain (see the next section), in conjunction with your knowledge of resource types and key capability or core competence identification. Questions are most likely to be related to internal strategic development or the external acquisition of key resources. Here is an essay question more specifically on resource management:

2 *What are the critical success factors in the market segments in which Nokia competes? How do Nokia's competences compare to these?*

This question requires you to first identify the major industry and market segments in which Nokia competes, the major rivals and why they are successful in their markets. Evaluate the critical success factors by identifying which resources are merely threshold and which ones are key capabilities or core competences. Use the resource analysis checklists and VRIO frameworks to help you here. Undertake the same exercise with Nokia to determine the competitive strength of Nokia in comparison to the requirements of the market.

Textbook guide

COULTER: *Chapter 4*
JOHNSON, SCHOLES & WHITTINGTON: *Chapter 3*
LYNCH: *Chapter 6*
THOMPSON & MARTIN: *Chapter 5 and Part 1, Supplement 1*

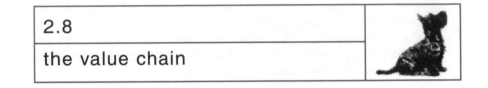

2.8

the value chain

As with the analysis of the external environment, frameworks exist to provide the strategic analyst with a methodological approach to evaluating the internal environment. Michael Porter (1985) provided the *value chain* tool which can be used with most organisational types, although with each organisation the emphasis and focus may be directed in different areas. It is called a value chain as value is added to the raw materials during the process of transformation to the final product. The aim of the organisation is, of course, to add sufficient value so that the customer is willing to pay a premium for the service or product and this assures profitability.

> *In many service organisations, value is added simply by responding quickly and efficiently to the customer's needs.*

If an organisation performs key functions cheaper or better than its competitors, then it will gain a competitive advantage. In the case of an organisation which is following a cost leadership strategy, the value chain will be optimised for high efficiency, low waste or re-work. In the case of an organisation following a differentiation strategy, the emphasis is likely to be on research, development and marketing.

The value chain may be divided into two halves, the *upstream* functions, which include inbound logistics and operations, and *downstream* functions, such as outbound logistics/distribution, marketing and service provision. Upstream value will be provided by low-cost *procurement*, efficient inbound logistics and operations; downstream value may be provided by advantageous R&D, effective marketing, competitive positioning and a quality service and support function.

As with any strategic analysis, it is not just a case of identifying the relevant factors – these must then be further analysed. In the case of the value chain, it is important to assess how well these activities are being performed. You might consider a particularly unique or effective link to be a strategic advantage or, if used widely across the organisation, it might be a core competence. The following are examples of the many questions that you should ask of the primary activities listed below:

- **Inbound logistics.** Is there an efficient inventory control system?
- **Operations.** What is the degree of automation and how well regarded are the quality systems? Is the factory running over- or under-capacity?
- **Outbound logistics.** Is there a reliable delivery system which assures stock in the right place at the right time? In a service organisation, this might include transporting customers to events.
- **Marketing and sales.** Is there a strong and effective brand management team? Are alternative sales channels and niche markets being investigated? Are there alternative customer communication channels?
- **Customer service.** What is the reputation in this respect? How are complaints handled? Is there a prompt repair or replacement process? What emphasis is placed on customer relationship management skills?

Likewise, from a support activities perspective, the following may be relevant:

- **Procurement.** Are the best prices obtained? Could the numbers of suppliers be reduced in order to maximise bulk purchasing opportunities? Are there beneficial long-term relationships with suppliers (enhanced communication and flexibility)?
- **Technological development.** How innovative is the company (e.g. the number of patents)? What is the percentage of revenue invested in R&D? Does the organisation foster a creative atmosphere (culture)?
- **Human resource management.** Are the employees motivated? Are key employees regularly leaving to join competitive organisations (high staff turnover)? Are there good labour relations (or union militancy)?

- **Firm infrastructure.** Are the value chain activities optimised for maximum efficiency? Perhaps with alliances to other partners? Is the IT system fully integrated in order to promote the dissemination of knowledge? Are the buildings in good order and sited optimally? Is there enough space to expand if necessary?

Not all these answers will be available to an outsider as much of it is company-confidential. However, it is important to look for clues in the information that you have in order to show that you are at least considering the importance of these characteristics. For example, hints about the introduction of a new IT enterprise system may indicate a weakness in the existing IT infrastructure, probably due in part to the incompatibility of existing systems.

You should use the value chain framework to deconstruct an organisation's processes to identify where cost and value might be created, start by looking for the following:

- The major stages (primary functions) in the production of goods or services.
- The supporting activities that provide the 'glue' for the primary functions.
- Look particularly at the interfaces between functions, for example, in retail organisations' outbound logistics (distribution) and sales.
- Identify if the organisation has a particular strength or weakness in any area. For example, the company might have a just-in-time (JIT) management system which improves links between inbound logistics and operations, or alternatively they may be carrying too much stock in their warehouse. Good product design and high-quality raw materials can reduce wastage and warranty costs elsewhere in the value chain.
- Determine if there are any beneficial links between the support and primary activities, for example, a reliable source of highly skilled employees.
- Look for links between parallel value chains (e.g. between products, where the organisation will most likely benefit from economics of scope). For example, look for the sharing of distribution networks or the same components in the manufacture of different models of cars.

Weaker students may just identify the stages of the value chain, but you have the opportunity to provide more detail and identify all the subtle links that make the difference. If you can subdivide each of the value chain stages into specific functions, see if you can identify a specific trait that benefits that section. Remember, any chain is only as strong as its weakest link.

You may find that not all organisational types fit neatly into the simple framework of the value chain. For example, the complete pharmaceutical value chain, from initial research to licensing, manufacture and delivery, may take more than ten years to complete, with multiple sub-stages at each primary segment.

Service organisations, such as banks and cleaning companies, bring their own issues as the services they provide are usually difficult to quantify except by time, they are not visible, they cannot be separated from the seller or provider, they are more difficult to standardise, they cannot be stored and the consumer does not own the service. These characteristics might make them difficult to fit into the value chain. However, service organisations do still require skills (and possibly other resources – inbound logistics), they create a service (operations), deliver the service (outbound logistics) and sell to and support the end-user.

> *An example of a lack of connectedness in a service organisation would be high expenditure on marketing and promotion in order to find new customers at the same time as losing high numbers of customers due to poor customer retention elsewhere in the value chain.*

Some service industries, such as the public sector industries, would 'classify' their products as their customers and promote customer relations because of this. Hence, in a hospital environment, patients would be 'processed' in much the same way as a product is manufactured. They might be brought into the hospital and register (inbound logistics), undergo an operation (operations!), spend time in a recovery ward and be taken home (outbound logistics). Follow-up with a local nurse or doctor (service) would complete the value chain.

Value chain networks

When considering the value chain, it is also important to consider the wider *value network* (also known as the value system) from the following perspectives:

1 The future value and competitive advantage that can be gained from the external relationship.

2 The opportunity to focus on the organisation's strengths with a view to outsourcing other activities.

3 The defensive strategy with the removal of a supply or distribution channel from the competition.

Many manufacturing organisations, such as Nissan in the northeast of England, have a tight relationship with their suppliers. Nissan's IT systems are linked in such a way that Nissan can track the movement of inbound raw materials (e.g. sheet steel) to its suppliers and then from its suppliers to its own production line. Clearly, this extended value network creates a competitive advantage by improving the efficiency of its own operations, minimising unexpected supply problems and creating a close working relationship with a whole range of key suppliers. This in turn may lead to a distinctive core competence.

In some instances, different organisations' value chains will share the same supplier or distribution networks. Tighter integration with one of these shared channels may enhance the relationship and at the same time reduce the effectiveness of the competitors' value chain.

Cost-efficiency, outsourcing and the virtual organisation

The value chain is an important tool in helping managers determine how and where value can be created (profit centre) and lost (cost centre). Different industries and sectors will have different cash-flow generation and expenditure points. For example, a manufacturing organisation is likely to have comparatively low labour costs compared to those of a service organisation; a retail chain will be concerned predominantly with stock control and outlet efficiency and a well-known brand will spend a significant proportion of its income on advertising. Costs can also come from the wider value chain network, such as supplier costs and through the organisation's competitive strategy.

Look here for links with Porter's five forces and the impact of buyer and supplier power, and the generic strategy of the organisation. For example, an organisation whose competitive strategy is focused on differentiation will spend proportionally more on R&D and marketing than an organisation following a cost leadership strategy.

Hamel and Prahalad (1993) suggest that an organisation can find value-adding opportunities by *stretching* or exploiting existing resources and knowledge, and should aim to *leverage* skills and technologies between products and business areas. In an organisation, this might include co-developing markets, the wider use of an in-house IT system, or even the creation of a new product or service from a specialist competence. An example of this is Unipart, which, after separation from British Leyland, moved from being a specialised automotive parts supplier with particular skills in logistics to a company providing complex logistics services to other companies, including Vodafone, Boots and Hewlett Packard.

Hamel and Prahalad (1993) have helpfully identified five methods by which managers can successfully leverage resources:

1   By focusing resources around key strategic goals.

2   By accumulating resources more efficiently.

3   By complementing one kind of resource with another.

4   By conserving resources whenever they can.

5   By recovering resources from the market place as quickly as possible.

Try to identify opportunities for stretch and leverage in organisations, as they are likely to improve efficiency and provide opportunities for strategic development in the future.

If an organisation knows its resource limitations, or suspects that the function is not cost-efficient, then it may be in a position to outsource this function of the value chain to other specialist organisations. This is particularly common with clothing retailers and electronics companies which concentrate on branding and retailing while leaving low-cost manufacturing to companies in the Far East. The pharmaceutical and agrochemical industries are also increasingly outsourcing research, development and safety testing in order to focus on manufacturing, licensing, distribution and marketing of the product, skills for which companies such as Aventis are best adapted.

Many service organisations are also *outsourcing* their call centres to cheaper parts of the world (also called *off-shoring*) where a high standard of education and a low wage provides the potential for large cost savings. However, other companies have witnessed consumer dissatisfaction that these outsourced centres sometime engender and now actively promote the use of UK call centres as a competitive differentiator.

> *Don't always assume that off-shoring automatically results in significant savings. Increasingly research has uncovered many examples of lower wages but also reduced productivity. Additionally, the costs of control and coordination of outsourced products and services or the impact on quality is rarely fully accounted for.*

In extreme cases, extensive or total outsourcing can lead to the formation of *a virtual organisation*, where a central team acts as a coordinator of all the other 'virtual' functions of the organisation. Industries such as publishing and civil engineering extensively outsource all their major functions, including those which might be considered core to their business. Other examples include Dell Computers and British Telecom, which seamlessly integrate virtual teams and other specialist organisations into their value chains.

A virtual organisation is a collaborative network of functions centrally coordinated using information and communication technologies (ICT).

There is no doubt that global and competitive pressures are increasingly moving organisations towards a virtual state. However, there are concerns that organisations which significantly outsource might benefit in the short term but at the expense of losing out on long-term innovation and core competence-building.

> *There are many important links here with the evaluation of alliance formation, joint ventures, vertical and horizontal integration and merger and acquisition strategies, in particular alliances with organisations that can provide a solution or the flexibility to outsource a weakness in the value chain. Alliances are discussed later in this Course Companion.*

Taking it **FURTHER**

> Don't just assume that service delivery may be good or bad and therefore a competitive advantage or not. In many organisations, and not just the not-for-profit organisations, service delivery can be a highly valuable part of the business. Companies such as IBM have strategically manoeuvred from providing computer equipment as their main source of income to consultancy and service provision as a key capability and basis of competitive advantage. Other companies make more profit from selling the disposable accessories than they do from selling the main product, for example, consumables for clinical equipment, or cartridges for printers. Indeed, the profitability of the consumable parts is sometimes so high that the main product is sold or rented 'at cost' in order to generate guaranteed revenue in the future.

EXAMPLE QUESTIONS

The scope for asking questions on the value chain is very wide. Example questions follow:

1 *Which of the following best describes why organisations are choosing to outsource value chain functions in order to create value?*

   (a) Outsourcing creates a leaner and therefore lower-cost organisation.
   (b) Outsourcing provides a way to focus on the value-adding core aspects of the business.
   (c) Outsourcing provides the opportunity to dispose of areas of the value chain that are unimportant.
   (d) External links allow for the flexible use of external experts.

While all of the above answers have an element of truth in them, answer (b) best describes the main driver for outsourcing non-core functions.

Internal analysis is most commonly asked for in an essay question as an addition to or an alternative to external analysis. You may be specifically asked to consider strategy with relation to the value chain or the development of the value chain over time, or possibly discuss how the value chain is used to the organisation's competitive advantage with specific reference to the organisation's resources. Here are some typical essay questions:

2 *Discuss the view that value chain analysis provides an appropriate frame-work to understand an organisation's strategic capability.*

This question is theoretical in nature and requires examples of where the use of the value chain analysis leads to specific identification of key capabilities or resources. The benefit of deconstructing the value chain has been discussed, in the previous section and could be used as a frame-work to your answer. The internal and external links of the value chain should be discussed, particularly where key nodes identifying a strength or weakness may occur. Don't forget to discuss the use of benchmarking competitive value chain networks, and the value of outsourcing and stretch and leverage in your discussions.

3 *Analyse Ikea's value chain, highlighting where value added activities enhance their competitive advantage.*

The answer to this question should not only detail all the key stages of Ikea's value chain but closely link these with Ikea's competitive advantage. A brief discussion of market segmentation and genetic strategies might be useful here. One of Ikea's competitive strengths is its low-cost structure, so you will need to analyse closely the stages in the value chain, from design to customer, to identify where efficiencies are made.

Textbook guide

COULTER: *Chapter 4*
JOHNSON, SCHOLES & WHITTINGTON: *Chapter 3*
LYNCH: *Chapter 6*
THOMPSON & MARTIN: *Chapter 5*

2.9

organisational culture

Every organisation has its own culture. It is formed from the beliefs, behavioural norms and values of its workforce and it is embodied in the structures, processes and strategies of the organisation. Analysis of the culture is critical to the understanding of how an organisation functions and may also influence the implementation of a new strategy. Clearly, new strategies have to be implemented and therefore require support throughout the organisation; an unsupportive culture will be a major hurdle to a successful implementation.

To analyse the main elements of *organisational culture,* it is important to first understand the impact of external and organisational factors. These include:

- the demographics of the organisation (e.g. age, gender, religion, education)
- the history of the organisation
- the size of the organisation
- the research orientation (basis of competitive advantage) of the organisation
- the cultural style of the organisation (power, role, task and personal)
- the strategic development (e.g. rapid or emergent).

The cultural web

One means to deconstruct many of these factors is to undertake a detailed cultural web analysis. This tool was developed by Gerry Johnson (1992) and is used in a similar manner to that of the PESTEL analysis in that it acts as a reminder of things to consider, but it can also be used in a number of other ways:

- It could provide the basis for a cultural analysis.
- It could be used to compare the organisation before and after change.
- It could be used to compare cultural similarities/dissimilarities of two organisations, possibly before a merger or acquisition.
- It can provide an impression of adaptability and willingness to change.

The key areas of the cultural web are as follows:

- **Stories**. What is talked about? Are there historical events that are significant?
- **Symbols**. What are the symbols of success?
- **Power structures**. Who makes the decisions and how are they influenced?
- **Organisational structure**. Is the hierarchy tall or flat? Is there easy access to senior people?
- **Control systems**. What is the degree of control? For example, is it performance orientated or bureaucratic?
- **Routines and rituals**. Are there special occasions marked by events?
- **The *paradigm***. This is a summary of what is culturally important to the organisation.

If we were to apply the cultural web to the company Google, the following might be the result:

- **Stories**. Google's founders, Larry Page and Sergey Brin, developed a new approach to online searching in a Stanford University dorm room in 1998. Desks were originally wooden doors mounted on sawhorses. IPO was through a 'Dutch auction' designed to give small investors a better chance of obtaining stock.
- **Symbols**. With rapid growth by word of mouth and the avoidance of corporate investment, it is the most used search engine, it provides high speed searches, it offers a simplistic layout with no inappropriate advertisements, and its headquarters are called the Googleplex.
- **Power structures**. It has a flat hierarchy and corporate decisions are made by significant shareholders and the founders, Larry Page and Sergey Brin. It has open plan offices with approachable executives.
- **Organisational structure**. Team-based working and the flexibility of workers to move to different tasks, for example, a programmer taking time out from his normal work to translate the website into Korean.
- **Control systems**. There are ten basic philosophies, including focus on the customer, do no evil, fast is better than slow, and being great isn't good enough. There are few rules and minimal supervision.
- **Routines and rituals**. There is a Google café and a 24-hour donut shop, its recreational facilities include exercise balls, piano, and roller hockey in the parking lot, there is no clocking in and out, the work must be done on time but it is down to the employee to determine how it is to be completed.
- **The paradigm**. Do no evil, do not settle for just being the best, support the democracy of the internet and have fun.

As a broad snapshot of the culture of Google, predominantly from Google's website, this quick analysis provides sufficient evidence to support the argument that Google is a creative and flexible company that is open to new ideas and opportunities. Because of this, it is unlikely to suffer from problems when implementing change, but the culture may not be helpful if there is a downturn in business resulting in cut-backs and tighter controls.

Google benefits from a strong positive culture built upon a diversified and flexible workforce and a willingness to do things differently. Strong positive cultures can be a competitive advantage because if positive traits are imbedded into the organisation, employees will need less supervision, will be more motivated and are more likely to be more flexible in their work practices.

> *Don't forget that culture is a form of control; a supportive culture can motivate employees to exceptional levels of performance.*

When analysing the cultural web, do not be surprised if some of the areas have less detail or some items appear multiple times. This does not matter as long as you have identified all the key themes. An ability to 'read between the lines' of your case study is often important here.

> *If an organisation has been regularly undergoing change and has shown itself to be flexible in the past, it is more likely to be supportive of a new strategy than one that is wedded to tradition, hierarchy, bureaucracy and the status quo.*

It is also important to recognise that large organisations might have differing cultures in different sections and departments, perhaps due to isolation or differing professional attitudes. However, what you are aiming to build is a general picture and feel for the organisation. This may be obvious, for example, if there is a history of militancy among the workforce, but it can also be subtle and may come from a single phrase which summarises 'the way things are done' in the organisation. A clue might be how people are treated after making an error – is there support and perhaps the offer of additional training or a threat of punishment?

When the organisation has grown very quickly, either by acquisition or rapid internal expansion, you should also consider if the dominant culture was diluted in this process, and whether all the 'new' employees had time to adjust to the cultural norms. Hewlett Packard is a commonly quoted example of a culturally unique company. However, few current employees would recognise the culture of the organisation as it was analysed ten or twenty years ago.

One thing to avoid is the temptation to take the vision or mission statement from the company literature and assume that all employees are aware of and in full agreement with the aspiration. Mission statements are sometimes more akin to a marketing tagline so it shouldn't surprise you that it may not bear any resemblance to the cultural reality within the organisation.

Cultural types – Handy

If it helps, also use the classifications of Charles Handy (1993) in order to identify the cultural types and differences based on organisational size and structure.

- **Power culture**. Most likely a small company dominated by one or only a few key people. The rate of strategic change is dependent on the style of the leader, who is most probably also the owner.
- **Role culture**. Relies on *bureaucracy*, scientific analysis and prescriptive decision-making. Probably hierarchical in structure, strategic change is likely to be slow and rational. Examples include government departments and large *multinational corporations*.
- **Task culture**. Work is team- and task-orientated, probably structured in a matrix format where strategic change can be fast if required. Examples include Google, Toyota and Hewlett Packard.
- **Personal culture**. Most commonly a professional organisation where individuals work according to their own goals and experience, and strategic change can therefore be instantaneous. Examples include firms of accountants and architects.

Linked to the above organisational types is the potential rate of change. Clearly, the larger, more traditional organisation is going to be less adaptable to change than a group of people who are used to flexible working and new projects.

Don't forget that several cultural types may exist in the same organisation, within different departments and countries, or even between different professional backgrounds. One way of breaking down these cultural barriers is to create cross-functional teams.

Taking it *FURTHER*

It is possible to examine organisational culture in some detail. Indeed, consultants make large sums of money undertaking cultural analyses in preparation to implement a change management strategy. A number of authors, including Charles Handy, have created extensive questionnaires which investigate in detail the history, management styles, communication styles and reward systems of organisations and their ability to accept change. Using this information, the consultant hopes to pre-empt any issues that might arise from cultural and strategic change.

EXAMPLE QUESTIONS

A multiple-choice question might be used to determine your understanding of the purposes of the cultural web, for example:

1 *Which of the following is not a good use of the cultural web?*

   (a) To determine whether the culture is supportive of change or not.
   (b) To provide a measure of employee satisfaction.
   (c) To compare the organisation before and after change.
   (d) To compare cultural similarities and dissimilarities of two organisations, possibly before a merger or acquisition.

Answer (b) is wrong. The cultural web does not provide a true measure of employee satisfaction, but it can provide an indication of whether change is likely to be acceptable and whether the culture is likely to be supportive of the business aims and objectives.

The following is a typical short-answer question of the sort that may be undertaken in a seminar session:

2 *Using Handy's cultural types, analyse the academic and student culture within your business school.*

The key thing here is to illustrate your answer with different examples of the learning experience. You might consider the library, students union, sports facilities and different forms of teaching, learning and assessment and relate these to Handy's cultural types.

Essay questions on culture may be specifically related to the subject or possibly combined with other aspects of internal analysis. If you are doing an examination and have the case study in advance, you might get a hint as to the level of detail the case study provides on the subject. If there is a heavy emphasis on the cultural aspects of the organisation, there is a good chance that you will be expected to analyse it!

The following question is an essay-style question and relies on the availability of detailed information:

3 *Using the cultural web, analyse the culture of Disney and compare it with that of Pixar Animation Studios. What are the key differences and how might the culture of Pixar be changed now that it has been acquired by Disney?*

This is a straightforward question which tells you to undertake cultural analysis of two organisations and compare them. The main emphasis will be the size and scale and structure of Disney in comparison to the relatively small Pixar Animation Studios. The conclusion might be that the relatively risk-averse tradition of Disney might smother the flexible and more risk-taking creative culture of Pixar. More alert students might identify that Steve Jobs (of Apple fame) is now a board member of Disney and may bring some of the Apple 'culture of design creativity' to the new organisation.

Textbook guide

JOHNSON, SCHOLES & WHITTINGTON: *Chapter 5*
LYNCH: *Chapter 7*
THOMPSON & MARTIN: *Chapter 7*

ORGANISATIONAL GROWTH

2.10	
growth and development	

Growth is desirable for any organisation and may be achieved by a number of means and measured in a number of ways. Organisations typically look for growth in revenues or profit, whereas not-for-profit organisations, such as charities, might look for an expansion in services or members, perhaps on a geographical basis (but are less likely to diversify). These strategies are formulated at the corporate level and the growth opportunities are summarised below:

1   Concentration in the same markets or with the same products.

2   *Diversification* into new markets with new products, for example, a food retailer diversifying into selling electrical appliances.

3   Expansion by *vertical integration*:

- forward integration (*downstream*), e.g. film producers owning their own cinemas.

- backward integration (*upstream*), e.g. a potato crisp producer acquiring potato farms to ensure a reliable supply and high-quality product.

4   Expansion by horizontal integration, which is usually with a competitor, e.g., the merger between Mobil and Exxon.

5   International expansion, for example, through foreign direct investment (FDI), e.g. investing in cut-flower production in Kenya.

Ansoff's methods of development

The first two options can be further divided and are summarised in the market/product matrix which is also commonly called Ansoff's growth matrix (Ansoff, 1988). These include the following options:

1 Concentration or exploitation of current markets with current products (also classed as consolidation, market penetration or protect and build).

2 New product development in current markets.

3 New market development with current products.

4 Diversification into new markets with new products (unrelated and related).

The concentration strategy is continually and most commonly used by organisations. Expansion by this method means that existing customers are retained, which is not just less expensive and less risky (the customer should be well understood), but it is also less likely to invite retaliation from a competitor. So long as the traditional markets continue to offer adequate growth, this option will be followed. It does not mean, however, that products do not undergo slight modifications or that target markets are not realigned in some way. They are also likely to require support through promotion, redesign or some other marketing activity which aims to stimulate an existing market. For example, air fresheners have undergone multiple changes over the years, with new packaging and many different ways to deliver fragrant smells to your room. However, the product, purpose and the target market are still fundamentally the same.

> You should also consider a concentration strategy as the pathway for consolidation. The business might withdraw from some markets and/or simplify the product portfolio in order to focus on its core business.

Expansion through the development of new products for the current market is used by companies to generate new streams of revenue from existing customers, particularly in markets such as consumer electronics where there is often a short product life cycle. Products in this category are usually quite different from the existing products but may still sometimes compete in some way with the existing product portfolio. Companies like Mars, for example, produce a large range of chocolate-based confectionary, much of it targeted at the same customers (i.e. the same consumer may buy a Twix, Snickers or a Mars bar). The introduction of a new product, such as ice-cream Mars bars, does, however, provide additional interest in the market and an opportunity to take market share from the competition. Similarly, many companies were, until recently, manufacturing both VCRs and DVD players for similar markets. Clearly, the DVD players were the newer technology which provided a succession of products by overlapping the product life cycles.

> If the products have some sort of commonality, such as using the same raw materials, production techniques or distribution channels, it may also provide the organisation with an opportunity for scale and scope economies.

Market development using the same products provides clear opportunities for scale economies. However, as with product development, it does carry some risk. By definition, new markets are often an unknown area for the organisation. Most organisations find that market entry is easier if the markets are rapidly growing, as the competitive rivalry may be less and customers may have no preconceived expectations. Finding a new market for existing products is a common way for companies to maximise their return on investment. New markets may be entered by finding:

- a new geography
- a new use for the same product (e.g. Aspirin as a painkiller but it may also be used to reduce the likelihood of blood-clotting)
- a new market segment (e.g. Vodka has been 're-invented' by creating small bottles with brightly coloured mixers that appeal to the youth market).

All of the above options are a means to expand the current core business and enable the organisation to build on its strengths. Diversification, however, requires expansion into new markets with new products in order to create a multi-business organisation. Of the growth alternatives, it is the most risky and organisations are only likely to undertake this route if there is a possibility that their existing products might become obsolete, the market is changing or there are limited opportunities for growth.

> **Note**
>
> If the launch of a new product into a new market is successful, then the organisation should benefit by spreading the risk of downturn across multiple businesses but will of course at the same time be placing less emphasis on its existing core business.

These contributing factors may well become evident from a PESTEL analysis. For example, a threat may be evident from a new health and safety law that is being introduced which means that a company's range of garden pesticides can no longer be sold. Similarly, as new technologies such as flat-screen TVs become available, it signals the end of the cathode-ray TV screens. Under these circumstances, so long as the organisation has recognised the signs, a pre-emptive action by diversifying into a new business is a possible solution.

> **Note**
>
> It is important to note that while diversification as a means of development is high risk, the alternative of doing nothing might be worse!

If an organisation pursues a strategy of broad diversification, often by acquisition, a *conglomerate* is formed.

Conglomerates are large companies that consist of multiple businesses commonly providing unrelated products or services.

General Electric (GE) is an example of a large diversified conglomerate that includes products such as financial services, plastics, security, aviation, transport systems, medical imaging, energy generation, healthcare and, through its ownership of NBC Universal, TV, films and theme parks. In such a diversified and unrelated portfolio, it is sometimes difficult to identify areas of complementary activity, which is why related diversification is preferable due to the increased likelihood of providing economies of scope.

> **Note**
>
> In the 1980s, diversified conglomerates were particularly popular with the stock markets but the fashion for diversification is less common and so only a relatively small number of large conglomerates still exist.

The concept of related diversification is often puzzling to students because if, for example, an organisation moves into a related market, then you might think that this would be similar to market development? This is true but it is a matter of degree. You should view 'related' as some form of connection with its existing technology, customer use, operational skills or the sharing of components in the value chain. The latter could be achieved by backward integration (upstream) into the supply chain or forward integration (downstream) into the distribution of products. The oil industry is vertically integrated in both directions, having vested interests in everything from discovering and pumping oil, through refining and retailing to the end consumer. Growth by related diversification has ensured that the oil industry has diversified its core business while at the same time achieving the benefits of value chain integration. The alternative development directions are illustrated in Figure 2.3.

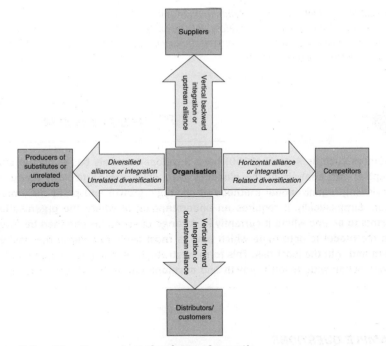

Figure 2.3   Direction and mechanisms of growth

Related diversification may also be by *horizontal integration*, which invariably means that the organisation has moved into a competitive or complementary area associated with its current activities. Returning to our original example, Mars has also diversified into vending drinks, pet foods and quick-cook rice. All are related in some way to their existing value chain and their core business of food production.

Ansoff's matrix (Ansoff, 1988) is a useful way to summarise the options that are available. However, it doesn't provide any means to determine which might be the most suitable direction of development. You should consider if one choice is better than another by considering the following criteria:

- Does the organisation have sufficient resources to undertake the growth strategy?
- Can the risk be minimised?
- Are there economies of scale or scope that might be achieved?
- Is there sufficient growth in the chosen growth option?
- Which is most likely to be the fastest route to achieving growth?
- Will the stakeholders support growth by this means?

Remember that high levels of investment might put some options out of reach of smaller organisations and may therefore only be an option for larger organisations. Also, some publicly owned service organisations will not have the remit or flexibility to consider alternative development.

Taking it **FURTHER**

Authors such as Argenti (1980) have developed models based on the concept of gap analysis or the planning gap, which are particularly useful in reviewing organisational methods of strategic growth and profit maximisation. Simplistically, it requires an understanding of where the organisation wants to be and where it currently is. A range of scenarios can then be fitted to the model to determine which path is most likely to achieve the desired aim and with the least risk. This form of strategic planning should be used in conjunction with Ansoff's growth and development matrix (Ansoff, 1988).

EXAMPLE QUESTIONS

As is often the case with multiple-choice questions, they are aiming to test your understanding rather than memory. There follows a question which demonstrates this.

1 *Which of the following provides the best opportunity for achieving economies of scale?*

    (a) Market development.
    (b) Product development.
    (c) Foreign direct investment.
    (d) Vertical integration.

Answer (a) is correct as it provides the possibility to sell more of the same product to additional or larger markets. The other options do not provide this opportunity.

Typical short-answer questions follow:

2 *Explain, using examples, why market development might provide scale economies where product development might provide scope economies.*

This question requires a discussion of market and product development and the opportunities for economies of scale with expansion of markets and economies of scope with related product diversification. The use of different examples provides evidence of wider reading.

3 *Illustrate, with examples, the advantages and disadvantages of conglomerate businesses. Explain why they are less common now than 20 years ago.*

The answer to this question provides the opportunity to discuss economies of scale and scope (see previous question) and the value chain and resource synergies. Look for at least one large conglomerate organisation on which to base your answer. Examples of complementary geographic coverage, shared production and distribution opportunities and possibilities for stretch and leverage of resources, technologies and skills should be given. A discussion of risk spreading and organisational control should also be included in your answer and a discussion of stock market fashions and *knowledge management* might also help you to pick up a few extra marks.

For an essay question, it is most likely that you will be asked to discuss the growth and development directions of an organisation rather than specifically asking you to use the Ansoff growth matrix. Read the question carefully as the emphasis may be on external growth (possibly by acquisition) rather than internal growth mechanisms (see next section).

4   *Critically evaluate the strategic growth of Siemens over the company's history.*

This is a typical case study essay question and provides the opportunity for the student to pull a wide range of information together. Start by creating a timeline of key events in Siemens' history and then relate each of these stages to the Ansoff matrix. This may be enough to get a pass, but for a high mark you should also elaborate your answer by using the strategic business terms that you have been learning. For example, if an organisation was acquired by Siemens, what were the benefits with regards to strategic growth? Was it a horizontal or vertical acquisition? Is it related or unrelated? And what were the complementary activities? You should compare the resources and cultures of all the external development that has taken place, and also look for useful alliances and the opportunity to use the terms 'stretch' and 'leverage'. Take your answer beyond the statement of the facts.

Textbook guide

COULTER: *Chapter 7*
JOHNSON, SCHOLES & WHITTINGTON: *Chapter 7*
LYNCH: *Chapter 13*
THOMPSON & MARTIN: *Chapters 9 and 11*

2.11

internal and external methods of development

Organisations can develop by internal and external means within their own country or internationally (international development is discussed in the next chapter). Organisations undergo *internal development* by building on their own resources and capabilities to develop products or services under their own control. The advantages of this means of development is that over time competences are developed and skills are retained. However, it may not be the fastest or cheapest way to market, and many organisations do not have the resources, skills, time or inclination to undertake development by this means. These organisations are more likely to expand by a means of *external development*, which may include one or more of the following types of cooperative venture:

- licensing and subcontracting
- strategic alliances
- franchising
- joint ventures and consortia.

Licensing and subcontracting

Licensing occurs when a product or service is used or manufactured by another organisation in return for the payment of royalties. Commonly, this will be based on intellectual property. For example, Pilkington Glass patented the float glass manufacturing technology and then licensed the process to other glass manufacturing companies, thus gaining global coverage. Likewise, brewers often license or subcontract the brewing of their branded beers to other breweries in order to gain access to foreign markets.

Strategic alliances

A strategic alliance is a partnership agreement between two or more companies to form a liaison that aims to reduce risk and achieve a mutually desired outcome. This form of external development has seen a massive growth in recent years, due to the increasing pressure that companies are under when competing in dynamic markets. Alliances may provide access to markets and resources, such as skills, materials and finance, which can be shared on an opportunistic basis or via a longer-term contractual or joint ownership basis. The airline industry, for example, has created networks of alliances, such as the Star Alliance, which facilitates ticketing, baggage handling, flight connection, use of airspace and so on to the benefit of the partners and customers.

Contract manufacturing and turnkey projects are also forms of strategic alliance. These are common in the manufacture of customised components or specialist buildings such as temperature controlled rooms. But they can also include large scale engineering projects such as dams or oil refineries; these are built and commissioned under contract prior to handing over to the alliance partner.

Other organisations might create alliances in order to enter new markets or to develop new technologies, especially when internal development would be considered as too slow, expensive or risky. Strategic alliances are also important in the public sector where the local focus and knowledge of a private organisation are matched to government funding, for example, in the case of social services and care for the elderly.

Franchising

If a strategic alliance is proven to be successful, then it may act as a precursor for a more formal relationship, such as a merger or acquisition.

Franchising is a form of licensing agreement where the parent company provides the franchisee with a package of resources, including technical help and marketing assistance. In return, the franchisor shares a portion of its profits with the parent company. This is particularly common with service providers in the fast-food and restaurant industry, for example, McDonalds, Subway and Pizza Express. Both licensing and franchising offer a fast means of expansion while minimising risk and financial outlay. However, losing control of intellectual property or risking damage to the brand's reputation is a common concern with these forms of expansion.

Joint ventures and consortia

Unlike a strategic alliance, a *joint venture* or *consortia* results in the formation of a new company which is jointly owned by the parent companies.

This may involve two organisations, for example, Sony and Ericsson, which created an equal joint venture to co-design and manufacture mobile phones. Sony provided most of the consumer electronics expertise and Ericsson the technological leadership in mobile communications.

Alternatively, multiple organisations may form a consortium such as the European Airbus, which was created with the financial support of several European governments in order to create a European passenger aircraft manufacturer to rival that of Boeing. Without government backing, the risk and financial barriers to entry were likely to have been too high for the individual companies.

Note

Public sector organisations also form consortia with private companies (Public Private Partnerships, PPP) in order to gain funding. Typically, a hospital might be built by a private developer and then leased back to the health authority. The private investor then acts as a landlord.

Figure 2.4 highlights the increasing levels of legal and resource commitment to the differing forms of external development and relates them to the less risky but typically slower methods of internal development.

An organisation may grow and develop by any of the above means, judging each expansion opportunity as being relevant for a particular market or product. Indeed, it is not uncommon for some large organisations to maintain tens of strategic alliances and more than one joint venture.

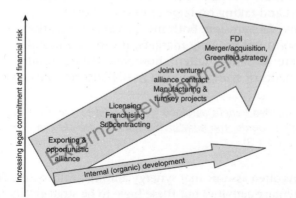

Figure 2.4 Development and growth opportunities via different forms of alliance

The more complementary the resources and skills are, the more beneficial the arrangement is likely to be. Trust and openness are also crucial and many joint ventures and alliances have failed due to miss-set expectations and strategic and cultural differences.

There are two further means of growing, by *merger* or *acquisition*.

A merger is the mutually agreed joining of two similarly sized companies to form a new company. Shares in the new company are distributed to all previous shareholders.

An acquisition or takeover is the outright purchase of one organisation by another.

Once acquisition has occurred, the company may or may not subsume the smaller company into its corporate structure; it may instead allow it to continue trading under its own name, as Disney did when it bought Pixar Animation Studios. This is a consideration if the purchased organisation already has a strong brand presence in the market, the parent company doesn't want to disrupt a positive culture, or the intention is to allow separate trading with a view to selling at a later stage.

Acquisition may be with the aim to gain control of brands, technology, core competences, and market share, or indeed for any of the product/market matrix development reasons. Acquisitions can be hostile or friendly. If hostile, defensive strategies may be used by the target to make the purchase less palatable to the larger company, for example, by buying assets and taking on large amounts of debt.

As a means of expansion, both mergers and acquisitions are relatively quick, and so in fast-growing markets, it can be a useful means to gain an immediate presence. Often, however, failure results because the expected benefits or *synergies* do not materialise and differences emerge.

Synergy is the added benefit obtained from joining two or more organisations together. In other words, the sum of the parts is greater than the individual contribution (1 + 1 = 3).

Organisations often assume that synergy automatically comes from related or complementary activities but these have to be strategically managed in order to maximise the opportunities from the merger or alliance. A recent example of this is DaimlerChrysler which, after nine years of troubled trading, split, with the sale of Chrysler to a private equity firm. The common reasons for failure of mergers or acquisitions are listed below:

- Cultural and structural differences hinder integration.
- The anticipated scale or scope of economy is not achieved and synergies are hard to develop.
- The price paid was too high, perhaps due to an artificially inflated share price at the time of the merger/acquisition.
- Frequently, it takes longer than expected to integrate the companies, especially in the case of cross-border mergers (see section on Internationalisation).
- Due diligence (prior investigation) may not uncover many of the cultural, structural, process and human resource issues which come to light after completion.
- The dominant company smothers or loses key creative skills, thus removing the original reason for purchase.
- The merger or acquisition was driven by personal greed and ambition rather than strategic logic.

When evaluating the mechanisms for external expansion, look for the benefits that it might bring to the organisation and ask why it has chosen to follow that particular route. As an aid, you might find it useful to ask yourself the following questions – they will help to define the likely reasons and probable success of the venture:

- Why did they create an alliance, joint venture, merger or acquisition?
- What does each partner bring to the table?
- Is there a well-defined strategic purpose?
- Are there clearly defined targets and performance outcomes?
- Are there mutual benefits and opportunities?
- Are there structural and cultural differences that may cause problems?
- Is one partner dominating and controlling the process?
- Are there complementary competences rather than identical ones?
- Are there likely to be synergistic benefits? If so, where?
- Is the price paid in line with the potential gains?
- In the case of private companies, has the share price increased or decreased since the announcement?
- In the case of public companies, have these organisations been in a previous alliance?
- Have they performed a thorough due diligence?

Contractor and Lorange (1988) identified the common reasons or factors that are behind any form of cooperative venture (including joint ventures, strategic alliances and mergers) and the following list is adapted from their work and includes examples of the benefits that might be acheived:

1 Competition

- Access to customers (buying market share)
- Access to brands
- Elimination competitor

2 Human/stakeholder

- Shareholder pressure
- Executive ambition

3 Entry into markets

- Access to geographical markets (including overseas)
- Avoidance of trade barriers

4 Accounting/financial

- Size and stability (including the reduced likelihood of takeover)
- Business diversification to reduce exposure (including seasonality)
- Avoidance of tax liabilities
- Use of spare cash (including 'poison-pill' action)
- Increase in speed of growth (including *first mover advantage*)
- Intention to asset strip

5 Product

- Access to products
- Diversification of product range

6 Efficiency/capacity

- Use of excess or gain in capacity in supply chain
- Synergy necessary to optimise economies of scale or scope – cost reductions

7 Resources/competences

- Access to resources (including technology and skills)
- Access to supply and/or distribution channels

As an aid to memory, you might notice that the first letter of each category spells CHEAPER. Each of these factors can be ranked and plotted based on the relative importance to each company involved in the cooperative venture. Figure 2.5 shows an example of two hypothetical companies. When graphically displayed, you can identify differing reasons behind the deal. Anything to the top and right of the chart will be important for both companies, but you may also see other clusters of interest depending on each company's perspective.

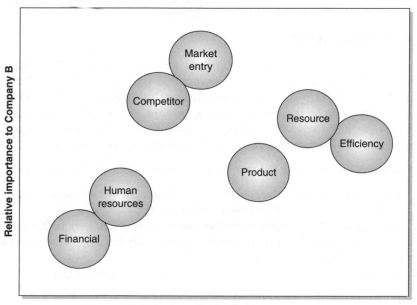

Figure 2.5   Key factors influencing an alliance, joint venture or merger

In the case of Company A, gaining efficiency, resources and access to new products are the most important factors; Company B is primarily looking for market entry, access to resources and removing a competitor as the primary drivers. Gaining additional skills or some sort of financial benefit was low on the list of reasons for both companies.

Taking it **FURTHER**

> It is important to recognise that the majority of merger and acquisition activity occurs in the UK and the USA due to the 'open-market' nature of share trading within these countries. This does not mean that mergers and acquisitions do not occur elsewhere but the involvement of banks, governments and cross-shareholding makes the process of merger and acquisition more difficult. Under these circumstances, the use of subcontracting and alliances provide flexibility without shareholder intervention or long-term commitment. If competitive or horizontal integration occurs, then the *Federal Trade Commission* (FTC) in the USA or the *Competition Commission* in the UK, might investigate to ensure that consumer choice is not being compromised.

EXAMPLE QUESTIONS

Questions on international development are popularly asked in multiple-choice and short-answer papers. However, recognition of the important factors of each form of growth, and the reasoning and logic behind the decision to grow by these means, are important in your understanding of wider case study strategic analysis. Examples of multiple-choice, short-answer and case-study questions on this subject are provided below.

1   *What is the difference between a joint venture and a strategic alliance?*

  (a)   A joint venture is the collaboration with a competitor whereas a strategic alliance is collaboration with a partner.

  (b)   A joint venture results in the formation of a new company jointly owned by the parent companies, while a strategic alliance doesn't form a separate company.

  (c)   A joint venture is the American term for a strategic alliance.

  (d)   A joint venture is the joint funding of a new company, whereas a strategic alliance just contributes skills.

The answer is (b), as a new company is formed with a joint venture; a strategic alliance doesn't create a new company.

2   *Providing examples, what are the advantages, disadvantages and differences between licensing and franchising?*

The answer to this question can be found in the previous section, and you should use different examples to illustrate your point. A discussion of the control of standards and the protection of intellectual property should be included.

3 *Critically discuss the benefits and limitations of internal development in comparison to external methods of development.*

The answer to this question is predominantly based around the benefits of speed in the case of external development or the control of information and skills if the product or process is developed internally. You should mention the alternative types of external development, the presence or absence of resources and previous development experience of the organisation. An evaluation of cost and risk should also be considered.

4 *Critically evaluate the logic of the mergers and acquisitions and alliances that the Tata Group has undertaken to-date.*

This is a common form of essay question. It requires a timeline of all the external growth events in Tata's history to be linked to a discussion of the anticipated benefits of each activity. You should identify the synergistic benefits and potential pitfalls of each development direction. Use the questions that are provided in the 7 point list in the previous section to help frame your answer. This question also provides an opportunity to use the terminology of Ansoff's growth matrix. Could an acquisition be classed as related diversification? If so, why?

Textbook guide
COULTER: *Chapter 7*
JOHNSON, SCHOLES & WHITTINGTON: *Chapter 8*
LYNCH: *Chapter 13*
THOMPSON & MARTIN: *Chapter 12*

2.12

internationalisation

Internal or external development can be equally applied on an international scale and these market entry strategies can also be mapped directly on to Ansoff's market development options. However, expanding internationally provides both new opportunities and concerns.

The opportunities of internationalisation include the following:

- It provides a means of growth – particularly if the local market is maturing.
- It enables exploitation of competitive advantages.
- There is the potential for scale economies and global sourcing.
- It might lower operational (e.g. taxation or labour costs) or transportation costs.
- It leads to improved organisational knowledge and learning and therefore enhances the innovation capabilities of the organisation.
- It spreads revenue risk by stabilising earnings across multiple countries.
- It reduces seasonality.
- It opens up the possibility of government incentives or opportunities for international alliances.
- It removes or bypasses a barrier to entry.
- It utilises excess capacity.
- It extends the life cycle of a product or service in a less developed market.
- It provides a common platform of service to international customers.
- It enables financial gains from doing business in multiple currencies or under different accounting regulations.

The concerns of internationalisation are:

- financial risk, including taxation and currency fluctuations
- increased control and coordination complexity
- increased risk due to lack of knowledge of markets
- increased exposure to environmental (PESTEL) factors (e.g. security risks)
- unknown competitor reaction
- infrastructure limitations (e.g. transport and communication)
- national cultural differences
- barriers to entry
- knowing which locations provide the most favourable risk/reward opportunity.

International market entry strategies and structures

In order to test the new market, an organisation might first undertake a low-risk internationalisation strategy, such as *exporting*, selling through the internet or through agents/distributors, licensing, franchising or creating a small overseas subsidiary. Exporting may be a useful mechanism to evaluate the market potential, but it might not be satisfactory due to:

* transportation costs
* import duty
* difficulties in managing the agent or distribution channel
* being remote from the consumer
* concern over the loss of intellectual property.

However, if exporting is successful, it may provide a springboard for further overseas development, possibly through licensing, franchising or *foreign direct investment (FDI)*. This would result in a staged international expansion.

Foreign direct investment is the long-term investment in assets in another country.

Note

FDI is more than just manufacturing in a low-cost country. It is also about optimising volumes on an international scale in order to reduce costs.

International development provides a number of structural opportunities which will be influenced by the corporate strategy the organisation wishes to undertake. These are often categorised as follows:

1 **Multi-domestic/multinational approach**

* Decentralised decision-making, low level of integration
* High local market responsiveness
* Examples include consultancy services and breweries

2 **Global approach**

* Centralised decision-making, high level of integration
* Low local market responsiveness (global standardisation)
* Examples include global brands such as Intel, Nike, Boeing and Starbucks

3 **Transnational approach, the formation of transnational corporations (TNCs)**

- Coordinated global approach to decision-making and integration
- High local market responsiveness
- Examples include cars, pharmaceutical formulations and financial services

The multi-domestic approach will best suit markets which are internationally different and where the organisation will wish to differentiate itself in each market. The global and transnational approaches are concerned with some degree of exploiting low-cost advantage through standardisation and the integration of activities. The *transnational corporation* is less rigid than a global one as it does provide for some flexibility in differentiating products in local markets.

> *Transnational organisations aim to optimise the advantages of both the multi-domestic and global approaches.*

When you apply the terms multi-domestic, global and transnational, you might find it difficult to neatly put the organisation into one category. This is because most large multinational organisations implement a range of these structures depending on the product, industry and market. Indeed, even organisations such as McDonalds, which is widely considered to be a global organisation, find themselves adapting their standard menu for local tastes. Categorisation might also be difficult as adaptations to local markets might be minimal, such as optional languages on an electronic gadget or changing packaging for each locality. In these cases, some centralisation and scale of economy may still be obtained.

Globalisation drivers – Yip

You might find it useful to consider George Yip's (2003) globalisation strategic levers as these will help you to decide whether the organisation is multi-local or truly global, or more probably somewhere in between!

- **Market participation**. There is a choice of countries in which to conduct business. Does the country have a profit potential in its own right? If so, it may be a multi-national organisation. Or does the presence in a country only make sense from a global perspective?
- **Products/services**. Is there a high degree of standardisation or are the products/services adapted for each market? Watch out for minor adaptations of a globalised standard such as on electrical items.
- **Location of value-adding activities**. Is the R&D, operations, etc. strategically located in key global markets, or are they replicated in each region as is more likely in a multi-domestic organisation?
- **Marketing**. Is there a globalised brand and advertising strategy or are they heavily adapted or changed for each locality?
- **Competitive moves**. In globalised organisations, competitive strategy is most likely to be applied across all regions rather than undertaking a series of unrelated strategies in different markets.

According to George Yip (2003), the pressures or drivers for globalisation come predominantly from four sources. These groupings are critical to the industry, however, they are not generally influenced by worldwide business.

1 Market pressures

- Are consumer requirements similar around the world? Is there a global convergence of tastes?

- Are there industry standards which apply globally?

- Are there appropriate channels of distribution?

- Is there a move to develop global advertising?

- Is there increased travel creating global customers?

2 Competitive pressures

- Are competitors operating on a global rather than a national scale?

- Do competitors have dominance in markets or supply and distribution channels?

- Is there increased ownership of corporations by foreign acquirers?

- Are there increasing numbers of global strategic alliances?

3 Government pressures

- Are governments deregulating markets and encouraging investment?
- Is there increased privatisation in previously nationalised industries?
- Are there opportunities to benefit from particular skills or resources?

4 Economic/cost pressures

- Are there opportunities for economies of scale in manufacturing, branding, R&D, etc.?
- Are there high levels of investment which need to be recovered?
- Do costs need to be reduced by seeking low-cost labour sources?
- Is there global sourcing of raw materials or energy?

You should consider these pressures for globalisation and make a judgement on whether a multi-domestic strategy is more appropriate than a transnational or global strategy.

It is best to treat each strategic business unit separately when conducting this analysis, otherwise the picture will be too complex and possibly misleading.

A useful way to graphically demonstrate the relative importance of each driver is to plot them on a scaled chart. A hypothetical example is shown in Figure 2.6.

Figure 2.6 demonstrates how charts can be used to provide a visual comparison of the key influences on globalisation between different industries. On this occasion, Industry 1 is under more pressure to globalise than that of Industry 2.

Location

A critical decision for any multinational organisation will be where to locate their international facilities. Factors such as the availability of low-cost labour, suitable skills and resources, low taxation and proximity to

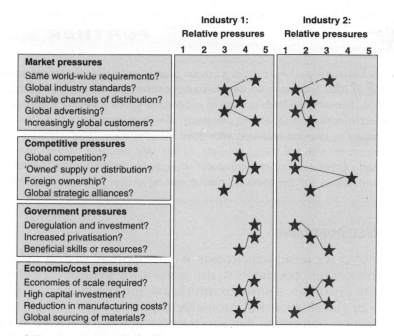

Figure 2.6   A star chart showing the relative importance of each globalisation driver in two different industries

the customer are all key considerations. Many transnational organisations choose to manufacture labour-intensive components in areas where labour costs are low. Final assembly might occur elsewhere and include customisation to the local needs. Bulky products, such as cement, are most likely to be manufactured close to where they are needed.

Don't forget that a corporate strategist will not only be considering the type of market entry strategy but also the degree and stages of a phased expansion.

There are numerous examples of multinational companies which have internationalised too quickly and too broadly, resulting in being over-stretched and perhaps being located in markets which they do not fully understand. This usually results in a retraction, consolidation and refocusing on core markets. For example, Marks and Spencer reversed its strategic decision to broaden its geographical coverage and withdrew from continental Europe.

Taking it ***FURTHER***

> Many transnational organisations create centres of excellence for manufac-turing or R&D and these act as knowledge centres for the rest of the organ-isation. Typically, the R&D centres of excellence will be linked to a particular research institute or a leading university. Similarly, manufacturing sites will be based in low-cost locations with good infrastructure, local suppliers and transport links to the target markets. In this way, business clusters may be formed. Examples include computer companies in Palo Alto, California (Silicon Valley) and the footwear manufacturing cluster in Wenzhou, China.

EXAMPLE QUESTIONS

This subject is a useful complement to other forms of strategy questions as it provides the opportunity to also evaluate the strategic logic of inter-national expansion. Questions which ask for the evaluation of the degree of globalisation will invariably require the use of Yip's (2003) globalisation framework, but also consider how your PESTEL analysis and Porter's five force framework might help in your evaluation. However, do not just analyse using your chosen frameworks, but evalu-ate what your findings mean to the organisation. In particular, give examples of where products or services have been adapted for different international markets and why this was and what impact it might have on the organisation. Example questions are provided below.

1 *Which of the following is not a feature of a global organisation?*

   (a) *Standardised products or services.*
   (b) *Being coordinated centrally.*
   (c) *High market responsiveness.*
   (d) *High level of integration.*

Answer (c) is not a feature of a global organisation. The main features of a global organisation are standardisation, centralisation and a high level of integration with minimal responsiveness to specific markets.

2 *Using examples, describe why a transnational approach to internationali-sation might be preferable to that of a global approach.*

Unlike the first question, this answer should be based on the subject of acting globally and thinking locally. Use the definitions of the different structures to frame your answer, illustrating with suitable examples.

3 *Critically evaluate the extent to which the industry and markets in which Electrolux operates might be regarded as global. Your evaluation should be based on an analysis of the industry and its markets.*

Evaluate both the industry and markets of Electrolux using Yip's globalisation levers and drivers. Your answer should be influenced by a targeted PESTEL, Porter's five forces and market segmentation analysis. Select the main impacting factors which are likely to influence Electrolux's global strategic decision-making. Determine where its R&D, manufacturing and centres of excellence are and why they have been positioned in these geographies.

Textbook guide

COULTER: *Chapter 7*
JOHNSON, SCHOLES & WHITTINGTON: *Chapters 2 and 8*
LYNCH: *Chapter 19*
THOMPSON & MARTIN: *Chapter 13*

CHOOSING AND IMPLEMENTING YOUR STRATEGY

2.13	
choosing your strategy	

SWOT analysis

Having undertaken an internal and external analysis of the organisation or industry, and considered the domestic and international development opportunities, the strategic status can be summarised. Students are often encouraged to do this in tabular form; Kenneth Andrews (1971) developed the SWOT matrix to show the key strengths and weaknesses from the internal analysis, the opportunities and threats from the external analysis and to provide a platform to develop strategic options.

As discussed earlier in this Course Companion, strategic opportunities exist when there is a good fit between the environment, values and resources (E–V–R congruence). Threats that become apparent from your analysis may be countered by using the organisation's resources and culture (values) to good effect.

Completing a SWOT matrix should be a relatively simple exercise as the hard work of analysis is already completed. Figure 2.7 summarises the main tools and frameworks to use for each category.

Strengths and weaknesses	*Opportunities and threats*
Internal analysis:	*External analysis:*
Resources: Financial, human, physical, structural, strategic capability/VRIO analysis, benchmarking, competences	Macro environment: PESTEL analysis, Porter's diamond
	Micro environment: Porter's five forces
Value chain: Efficiencies and inefficiencies, value network, outsourcing, stretch and leverage	Competitive environment: Strategic group, competitive analysis, Porter's generic strategies, Bowman's strategy clock, four links cooperation model, BCG portfolio analysis
Culture: Cultural web analysis	Growth opportunities: Ansoff's methods of development, international market entry, Yip's globalisation drivers

Figure 2.7 Analytical tools and models commonly used to create a SWOT table

When completing a SWOT analysis, it is also important to consider the competitive position as this often has more relevance than just looking from an organisational perspective. For example, many managers and companies blandly claim that their product performance is undoubtedly a strength, however, when competitively benchmarked, a feature that was previously considered to be a strength could actually prove to be a relative weakness.

When evaluating your SWOT analysis, try to find things that are potentially a threat but which may also be managed as a future opportunity – in other words, turn a weakness into a strength. For example, you might consider that a weakness is a product that is launched late to the market, however this may also be considered a strength if the design has since overcome the limitations of the competitors' products, as well as incorporating some newer competitive features.

Students often make the mistake of listing too many factors in each category with no real attempt to identify or rank their importance. A good SWOT analysis will identify no more than three or four relevant factors in each category and provide supporting evidence for each.

There are almost unlimited factors that could end up in a SWOT matrix and each organisation will have its own individual profile. Figure 2.8 provides an example SWOT, although you wouldn't normally expect to see all of these appearing in the same table!

Internal strengths	Internal weaknesses
• Gaining market share	• Staff resistant to change
• Stable cash flow	• Products not sufficiently differentiated
• New product time to market	• Poor organisational structure and control
• Service quality (benchmarked?)	• Old manufacturing facilities
• Good network relationships	• High cost base
External opportunities	**External threats**
• Growing markets	• New competitor
• Good national infrastructure	• Limited growth in current markets
• Change in legislation	• New substitutes
• Weak competitors	• New barriers to trade
• Low-cost sourcing	• Increasing labour costs

Figure 2.8   Some factors that may appear in a SWOT analysis

Once you have identified all the important factors relating to the organisation, you should ask yourself the following questions:

- How can the organisation overcome weaknesses?
- How can the organisation overcome threats?
- How can the organisation exploit their strengths?
  - Will it also overcome a threat or a weakness?
  - Is there a new market where this can be achieved?
- How can the organisation maximise their opportunities?
  - Will it also overcome a threat or weakness?
- What new growth opportunities are there?

When answering these questions, you should link your findings and considerations back to your strategic analysis, provide evidence of your rationale and start to evaluate possible future strategies for the organisation. For example, if you found that a ban on alcohol advertising is imminent and is likely to adversely affect alcohol sales, make sure that it is identified in your PESTEL analysis and look for an opportunity to neutralise the threat by building on the organisation's values and optimising its resources. Perhaps look to other industries, such as the tobacco industry, to see how they have managed similar legislation.

Taking it *FURTHER*

> One of the many limitations of the SWOT analysis is that you may find that some of the strengths also appear as a weakness. For example, a large market share in a niche market is obviously a strength, but it is also a threat due to increased exposure to risk and limited growth opportunities. Examples like this should still be illustrated providing that you can support the case for both sides.

EXAMPLE QUESTIONS

In an examination, it is most likely that you will be required to complete a SWOT analysis as a summary section based on a previous broader study. However, it is also possible that you might be required to answer multiple-choice questions or be asked to discuss the advantages and disadvantages of using SWOT as a tool. These questions might be similar to the following:

1 *Which of the following best describes the purpose of a SWOT analysis?*
   (a) *It is an alternative to doing a PESTEL analysis.*
   (b) *It provides a list of priorities for the organisation to consider.*
   (c) *It summarises the capabilities, opportunities and issues with regards to the internal and external environment.*
   (d) *It summarises the strengths and weaknesses of the organisation.*

The answer is (c) as a SWOT analysis provides a summary list of the internal capabilities and weaknesses and external threats and opportunities. The other answers are inaccurate or incomplete descriptions of the purpose of a SWOT analysis.

2 *Critically debate the advantages and limitations of a SWOT analysis.*

Your tutor will be looking for a debate using real and current examples. Your answer should discuss the benefits as a means of summarising a broad range of external and internal information but also the limitations of being too simplistic. For example, it does not allow for benchmarking against the competition, factors can appear both as a strength and weakness and it does not provide the opportunity to rank the importance of each of the factors.

Textbook guide

JOHNSON, SCHOLES & WHITTINGTON: *Chapter 3*
LYNCH: *Chapter 13*
THOMPSON & MARTIN: *Chapter 4*

2.14	
suitability, feasibility and acceptability (SFA) of the strategy	

SFA analysis

We have completed our strategic analysis and by using the SWOT tool have identified a small number of strategic options that would benefit the organisation if implemented. However, an organisation rarely has the resources to implement all the required strategies simultaneously, and if it did, it may still not be the best solution. Hence, a process of rationalisation needs to take place in order to evaluate the importance and likely success of each of the strategies. There are many processes that may be followed, but one of the simplest evaluates the *Suitability*, *Feasibility* and *Acceptability* (SFA) of the proposed strategies.

- **Suitability** acts as a reassurance that the proposed strategy addresses the key issues that have been identified in the SWOT analysis. It broadly asks 'Does the strategy make sense?' The evaluation of this has largely been completed by the previous strategic analysis. All the previous external and internal frameworks should be used in order to help evaluate the suitability of the strategy in order to overcome the threat or weakness or to take advantage of an opportunity or strength. If relevant, growth opportunities should also be considered.
- **Feasibility** evaluates whether a strategy is likely to be successful. It looks at the implementation of the strategy and the availability of the necessary resources, including the availability of skills and finance.
- **Acceptability** evaluates whether the organisation's stakeholders are likely to support the new strategy and focuses on the returns and risk involved. Cultural awareness is also required (cultural web) in order to determine the likely acceptance of the strategy by the organisation itself.

Implementing a strategy involves change and change necessitates some form of risk, so a strategy must look promising from all of the three SFA perspectives. The evaluation of the suitability of strategy is rarely clear-cut. All the strategic options are likely to be suitable to some extent as each has already undergone a process of strategic evaluation. However, it is the degree of suitability that is important. Tools such as ranking, decision-tree modelling, game theory and scenario planning may all be useful in highlighting the respective advantages and disadvantages of each strategy. The following three questions might add some clarity to the decision:

1 Does the strategy add value (e.g. profit, customer satisfaction, etc.)?

2 Is it consistent with other organisational strategies (e.g. resource allocation)? Does it fit well with the mission of the organisation?

3 Does it improve the competitive advantage of the organisation (e.g. market share or provide additional resources in the case of non-competing organisations)?

As an example, when studying the value chain you may find duplication in development or distribution which will provide a value-added incentive to support the strategy. Alternatively, you might find that the organisation is competing on the basis of a focused differentiation strategy, but the new strategy proposes growth by international expansion and a low-cost strategy and because of this it may not be suitable.

> **Note**
>
> It is possible that the two strategic directions can be successfully developed but does it make efficient use of internal resources and competences?

When evaluating the feasibility of the strategy, you are considering whether the organisation has the resources and competences not just now but over the implementation period of the strategy. Financial analysis is obviously a key consideration here, with cash-flow forecasting and *break-even analysis* providing a useful perspective. However, a strategy is only viable if there are also the relevant skills and resources available. If during your internal analysis you have identified beneficial resources and skills that have already been demonstrated by the organisation, it may be possible to stretch or leverage these to support your strategy. For example, a *strategic business unit* (SBU) may have already undertaken a market entry strategy which may provide both the resources and experience that can be utilised when implementing a similar market entry strategy elsewhere in the organisation.

You should also be asking whether the organisation is lacking internal resources or commitment, or whether it can build on existing resources and competences. This may be as basic as not having enough suitably skilled employees to successfully implement the strategy, or failing to gain commitment from the management and employees to implement the strategy, perhaps due to previous labour agreements.

> *Also consider constraints that come from outside the organisation, such as the likely competitor, supplier or government reaction. For example, promising product launches have often met with disaster due to price wars breaking out, with the incumbent players showing a greater ability to maintain a profit while decreasing prices. Existing suppliers may not support the new products or services, or government regulations may mean that a planned merger has to be reviewed by the Competition Commission.*

Acceptability of the strategy is concerned with the relative risk and anticipated stakeholder reactions to the proposed strategy. If the strategy is unlikely to provide the anticipated financial returns relative to the effort and investment that is made, then clearly it may not be acceptable to the shareholders and other organisational stakeholders. Sensitivity analysis plays an important role here for risk evaluation, with profitability being most commonly predicted by *return on capital employed* (ROCE), payback period or *discounted cash-flow* (DCF) analysis. These calculations can be a useful comparative tool, providing a simplistic comparison of different strategies, and may identify those strategies with a preferable cost structure.

> *Be aware that any financial analysis is only as good as the numbers that are used and the assumptions that are made – at best, it will only provide one perspective.*

Major shareholders often have some influence over strategic decision-making and because of this organisations may make concessions in order to keep the share value and dividends as high as possible. Indeed, some companies actively *manage shareholder value* (MSV) in order to optimise shareholder returns. Depending on the company or industry that you are evaluating, you should consider the shareholder returns and look at the past history to determine if the stock markets have reacted in a volatile manner to similar strategies in the past. This is particularly the case when a company indicates a major shift in strategy such as large-scale redundancies or an acquisition proposal.

> *The support or otherwise of the stock markets acts as an indicator of the degree of acceptance for the proposed strategy.*

Clearly, most strategies are too complex to evaluate solely from a financial perspective. There are often major benefits to the organisation which are more intangible by nature. For example, foreign direct investment (FDI) may provide other advantages, such as development of organisational knowledge, broadening experience, opportunities for further expansion, new opportunities in the supply and distribution networks, providing employment opportunities in a deprived region, spreading risk, etc.

The problem from an organisation's perspective is that the intangible benefits are difficult to quantitatively value, which is why there is often a heated debate about the appropriate cost of an acquisition – the intangible potential can often contribute more to the cost than the value of the tangible or quantifiable benefits.

Stakeholders, stakeholder mapping, power and influence

Stakeholders are the individuals and groups who are affected by or impact upon the performance of the organisation.

Stakeholders may be categorised by many different means. For example, they may be classed as having a contractual or legal relationship, such as employees and suppliers, and those that do not, for example, pressure groups and the media. Alternatively, you may have been taught to categorise stakeholders as internal or external. In the end, it doesn't really matter so long as you have considered all the stakeholders and their relative importance.

Examples of stakeholders include government departments, shareholders, *non-governmental organisations* (NGOs), banks, suppliers, customers and employees. Influential stakeholders often have a key role in the acceptance or rejection of a strategy and because of this it is often useful to determine which stakeholder group or coalition has the most interest, influence or power with regard to the strategy in question.

Stakeholder mapping tools are useful for a more detailed analysis and they provide varying degrees of sophistication – some adding the perspectives of group networking and management legitimacy into the mix. A commonly taught mapping tool was originally developed by Mendelow (1991) and is called the power interest matrix. As a tool, what it lacks in sophistication it gains in simplicity.

When using the power interest matrix, you should classify the stakeholder groups according to their relative influence or power over the organisation and whether they are likely to take any action over the proposed strategy. Power may be achieved through having a control of resources (including finance, skills and knowledge), through informal or formal influence or by their status within the organisation. For example, an institutional shareholder may exhibit power by threatening to sell its stock, the employees by threatening to take industrial action, the media by bringing adverse publicity, etc.

Mendelow's power interest matrix has four categories:

1   **Minimal effort.** Low power and low interest (e.g. community groups).

2   **Keep informed.** Low power and high interest (e.g. employees).

3   **Keep satisfied.** High power and low interest (e.g. institutional shareholders).

4   **Key players.** High power and high interest (e.g. banks).

The examples used for each category will change according to the organisation that is being evaluated. For example, in a local not-for-profit organisation, the community groups may have significant power and interest as they often provide vital support. In other organisations, employees may be appropriately classified as 'key players', perhaps due to rigorous labour agreements or a history of militancy when changes to working practices have been proposed. For example, the Royal Mail is currently undergoing significant changes but is severely limited in its strategic aspirations due to strong employee power.

Also, consider including in the 'key players' quadrant external stakeholders, such as suppliers and the media. Under some circumstances, combined effort can exert significant pressure on organisations. For example, an environmental pressure group, currently in the 'keep informed' quadrant (2), may contact the media in order to raise the profile of their concerns, thus increasing their relative power and influence, which then moves them to the 'key players' quadrant (4). This was the case in 1995 when Shell planned to dump the *Brent Spar* oil platform in the North Sea. First, Shell viewed the campaign groups, which included Greenpeace, as a minor irritation, but with increasing media and public pressure across Europe, Shell eventually had to reverse its plans and dispose of the oil rig by other means.

> *Different countries have different rules of governance, ownership and employment laws. This may change the relative power of the stakeholders and may restrict the strategic options available to the organisation.*

While the purpose of stakeholder mapping is to anticipate potential blockers and facilitators of your strategy, it is how the organisation uses this information that is important. However, the situation is often changeable. For example, large groups of shareholders may initially support a strategy but can change to become blockers in the future. Also, some groups may exhibit high power, for example, they may shout a great deal but in fact they may just be a vocal minority with little real power. A recent example is a group of media-savvy protesters demonstrating against the environmental impact of air travel outside the offices of BAA at Heathrow airport. This did not cause significant disruption to the day-to-day function of BAA, but did highlight the issue to the world's media.

Note

Groups may contain a large number of members and are therefore unlikely to be homogeneous. This usually makes it difficult to categorise a diverse group under one heading. Nevertheless, try to build a generalised picture of the stakeholder map and the likely facilitators and blockers of the proposed strategy. In practice, it is rare that you can please all the stakeholders all the time and an element of risk and compromise often has to be undertaken in order to grow the organisation. For example, many organisations find that they need to provide reassuring promises such as a 'no redundancy guarantee', or even incentives in the form of future dividends in order to aid the acceptance of the strategy.

You might also want to consider how the organisation best maintains its relationship with the wider stakeholder network, whether simple regular written communication is sufficient or whether meetings and briefings are more appropriate. This will depend on the significance of the strategy, the importance of the stakeholder and the complexity of the message.

It is generally considered to be good business practice to be aware of the influence of the stakeholders on the organisation (and vice versa) in order to act as a good corporate citizen and to reduce conflict and risk at a later stage. In the late 1950s, when the M1 motorway was being constructed in England, the director of the project visited 300 homes which were to be affected by the new road. During and subsequent to the project's completion, there were very few complaints from these resident stakeholders – they had been kept informed of developments, had their concerns listened to and were an integral part of the project.

Taking it **FURTHER**

When considering not-for-profit organisations, the underlying belief systems will be a key determinator of strategic acceptance. If an organisation relies on voluntary staff, a good relationship has to be maintained as an inappropriate strategy can quickly alienate this vital resource. However, there will often be a difficult balance of priorities between service delivery, fundraising and profitability. For example, should a charity spend its donations on advertising or new buildings or by employing professional fundraisers? The NHS provides vital medical care in the UK, but there is always a trade-off between the available resources and the services offered. Under these conditions, does a hospital provide 20 hip replacements or four heart bypasses?

EXAMPLE QUESTIONS

A multiple-choice question on this topic may be phrased as follows:

1 *When evaluating strategic options, what is the purpose of the test for suitability?*
   (a) To determine whether the strategic option is suitable to be put to the stakeholders.
   (b) To evaluate if the strategic option provides the most appropriate solution to the organisational issue.

(c) *To determine if the strategic option fits the current strategies of the organisation.*

(d) *To evaluate if the strategic option is suitably risk-free and therefore might work.*

The answer to this question is (b). The strategic option must meet several criteria including providing a workable solution as well as fitting with existing strategies. The other answers are either inaccurate or too narrow in their description.

Essays on the subject of SFA are a favourite of strategy lecturers as they potentially include all the frameworks previously studied. A question may be phrased as follows:

2 *Using the available information and appropriate models, discuss the suitability, feasibility and acceptability of Northumbria police's chosen strategy.*

To answer this question, you need to undertake a full external and internal analysis to determine the suitability of the strategy in achieving the organisation's objective. For feasibility, ask yourself if the organisation has the relevant resources and skills, and in particular if there is a sufficient cash flow. Much of this information will be available as a result of your internal analysis. For acceptability, you will need to determine, through the use of stakeholder mapping tools, who the key stakeholders are and whether they are likely to support or reject the proposed strategy. The cultural web tool may also provide an indication of the level of acceptability and support for the new strategy.

With or without the use of stakeholder maps, your tutors are most likely to be interested in why you think that some stakeholders are more important to the organisation than others. A brief discussion of your reasoning often helps to clarify this. Don't forget to evaluate whether a stakeholder might become more powerful in the future by joining forces with other stakeholder groups. Questions specifically on stakeholders might include:

3 *Using Mendelow's power interest matrix, analyse the UK stakeholders of HSBC. Explain the reasoning behind your analysis.*

This question is very direct in its requirements. Points will be awarded for accurate reasoning behind the stakeholder classification in the matrix. Where you can, subdivide stakeholder groups in order to create a more accurate representation of the groupings, for example, consumers may be subdivided into business and private customers. You might find that some groups are difficult to place and perhaps you may feel that they belong in more than one category. This is OK but explain your reasoning. Don't forget the government, employees and financial regulators in your evaluation!

4 *Critically examine the notion that failure to address legitimate stakeholders can lead to organisational failure.*

This question does not require the use of a stakeholder map but does expect you to be able to list some relevant examples of organisations, preferably both private and public, that have not correctly anticipated stakeholder reactions. Most large organisations will provide useful illustrations for your discussions. Use these examples to demonstrate failure in otherwise successful strategies. It will also be useful to highlight the problems that the organisations had to overcome and the resulting damage to their image. What have these organisations learned from their experiences?

Textbook guide

JOHNSON, SCHOLES & WHITTINGTON: *Chapters 4 and 10*
LYNCH: *Chapters 12 and 14*
THOMPSON & MARTIN: *Chapter 11*

2.15	
implementing your strategy	

7-S framework – McKinsey

One of the many methods of building a cohesive and coherent strategy is to apply the 7-S framework. This framework was developed by McKinsey Consultants and shows the interrelationships between different aspects of corporate strategy. In short, it is a reminder of the seven key elements to consider when developing and evaluating a strategy.

1   Strategy – what is to be evaluated.

2   Structure – of the organisation.

3   Systems – organisational procedures.

4   Style – leadership and culture.

5   Staff – who need to change.

6   Skills – key capabilities or core competences.

7   Super-ordinate roles – values and mission.

Each of these aspects should interrelate with each other and each should have equal prominence despite some being more tangible than others. However, other key attributes have since been identified and should also be considered. These include:

- innovation
- knowledge
- customer service
- quality.
- unfortunately they don't begin with 'S'!

Strategy and organisational structure

We have evaluated and prioritised the strategic options and are now ready to implement our strategy. However, as highlighted by such authors as Chandler (1962), Galbraith and Kazanjian (1986), and Mintzberg (1990), new strategies often require a change in organisational structure. For example, following the merger between Hewlett Packard and Compaq, Carly Fiorina based her new corporate strategies around the customers' needs. This necessitated a global restructuring from that of product-orientated divisional structure to one that was customer- and market-focused. A restructuring such as this can mean that value chains may need to be modified, outsourcing may need to occur, or product development may require the cross-fertilisation of ideas by teams of specialists. In summary, an appropriate structure needs to be in place in order to allow for the following:

- effective vertical and horizontal communication
- efficient use of skills and resources (scope and scale economies)
- elexibility to adapt when necessary
- knowledge sharing and creativity.

From a practical perspective, the more standardised the task the more centralised, functional and controlled the organisation will be. For example, a company manufacturing in bulk will be focusing on its overheads and following a cost leadership approach which is carefully monitored and controlled. On the other hand, a more creative organisation, such as Google, is less centralised, more flexible and diverse, and uses fewer rules and controls.

Large organisations commonly control through a range of structures which are constantly changing according to the current chief executive or business fashion. In your research, evaluate the organisational structure and its appropriateness to the proposed strategy. Start by considering the following configuration and coordination choices:

- divisionalised structure or a network of alliances?
- accountability to the top versus horizontal integration?
- tight or loose control?
- centralised or devolved decision-making?
- standardised or localised development?

Look out for new products that are being developed within a separate division. This may be to keep a tight control on costs or to provide the flexibility to integrate or close it at a later date without greatly impacting on the rest of the organisation.

Don't forget the power of organisational culture as a means of control. Government organisations such as the UK Environment Agency may be a hierarchical bureaucracy but many of the staff are also driven by environmental ideologies, which have a positive impact on their work ethic.

Managing change

Implementing a new strategy often requires direction from the organisational leader, however change may also be incremental and implemented over a long period of time possibly from the bottom up. Change may also be broad or narrow, required quickly or implemented on a phased basis. You might find Julia Balogun and Veronica Hope Hailey's (1999) change matrix useful in identifying the type and scope of change that the organisation has undertaken. Many organisations will undergo periods of change that may be rapid and transformational followed by periods which are relatively stable and only require incremental changes. Fortunately, business analyst reports and case study notes will provide much of this information so it shouldn't require much research.

When undertaking a full analysis, you should attempt to link the types of change to one or more environmental influences, new business partners, new technologies or even a new strategic leader with new ideas.

A consideration of the degree of change is an essential part of any strategic evaluation and implementation. Lewin (1952) developed a three-stage model to explain the change process:

1 **Unfreezing the current attitudes.** The change is identified.

2 **Moving to a new level.** The change is implemented.

3 **Refreezing attitudes at the new level.** Change is supported by behavioural changes.

An example of a Lewin's three-stage model is the implementation of changes undertaken by Carlos Ghosn of Renault, who in 1999 was charged with saving Nissan from bankruptcy. The first stage of the change management process was the open discussion of the major problems of the company and the serious consequences that it faced. He then generated cross-functional teams drawn from all levels of the company to analyse each problem and to provide solutions. These solutions were then led and implemented by the same teams. The refreezing was achieved in part with reinvestment, open communication, performance-related promotion and other performance incentives.

> *Quite often, this whole process may take many months or years to fully implement and a great deal of effort and resources are required in order to maintain the momentum, otherwise the process could easily slip into reverse.*

This three-stage model is useful but it is often difficult to identify when the unfreezing and refreezing stages are reached as each stakeholder group is likely to provide a different perspective.

Resistance to change can be anticipated and should be proactively addressed. Many strategies fail due to the lack of support across the organisation and this is perhaps understandable if employees and managers feel that they are likely to 'lose out' in the new scheme. It is therefore vital to encourage and, most importantly, to explain the need for change and the consequences of doing nothing. During this process, key employees should also be encouraged not to leave as organisations often risk losing vital members of staff to their rivals under conditions of uncertainty.

> *A stakeholder map and evaluation of those groups who may resist and those who may support change can provide a useful backdrop to this evaluation.*

Lewin (1952) also provides us with a force field analysis model which provides an insight into the strategic changes that are required and possible areas and reasons for resistance. Usually, the reasons for change are logical but resistance is often the result of basic emotions that include pessimism, anxiety, irritation, lack of interest, personal ambition, perceived loss of power, etc. Understanding the politics of the organisation in conjunction with these basic emotions can be a useful guide to identifying how to overcome the resistance. Figure 2.9 highlights some of the force field issues in the case of the Nissan–Renault alliance.

Despite the seemingly daunting list of resistance factors, these were carefully managed and the financial turnaround of Nissan is widely regarded as being very successful.

> *You might wish to consider the process of overcoming resistance as a 'stick or carrot' approach – a 'stick' to persuade or a 'carrot' to encourage. A 'carrot' might include performance bonuses, awards or promotion; the ultimate sanction, or 'stick', may be the threat of redundancy.*

Company for	Employee concerns
• Increased efficiency	• Closure of factories and job losses
• Reduced costs	• Impact of cheaper parts on quality
• Increased motivation	• Loss of promotion/status
• Increased accountability	• Increased commitment
• Dismantling of *Kieretsu* for capital	• Is the future secure?
• Senior management being predominantly from Renault	• Renault taking over – Nissan culture ignored

Figure 2.9   Force field analysis after the Nissan–Renault merger

Some less drastic and otherwise helpful mechanisms to encourage change might also include:

- using appropriate and regular communication
- gaining the full support of middle management
- providing incentives such as bonuses (however, if the intention is to motivate, financial incentives are rarely successful on their own)
- creating cross-functional teams to work on new projects to break down old barriers and create a sense of ownership
- empowering, educating, retraining and re-skilling employees
- using symbolic changes, such as a new logo, to act as a reminder that change has happened
- rewarding 'good behaviour' (e.g. by linking personal development with strategy implementation)
- identifying powerful antagonists and planning ways to win over or undermine their efforts, possibly by withdrawing resources from them
- restructuring, which can disrupt resistance and also signal change
- identifying influential supporters throughout the organisational ranks and establishing a *change agent* network.

A change agent is anyone who is charged with supporting the implementation of the strategy and identifying potential implementation problems. Typically, change agents are either employees or external consultants.

If you are asked to evaluate the change process in an organisation, look for clues (starting with the above list) in the communication styles and restructuring process to see if you can identify who the change agents might be. If the change is a transformational one which needs to be implemented quickly (i.e. big bang), you can expect to see a direct approach with major structural changes, possibly with the closure of sites, large-scale redundancies and other cost-cutting measures. If the change is more incremental in nature, look for new performance-related bonus schemes and identify what they relate to and how they might support the change process. Some powerful stakeholders may leave, others may have to be 'bought off' and others may be supportive. See if you can categorise who these might be and how well the organisation managed the overall change process.

When studying change management, your tutors might also discuss with you the change options matrix which helps to identify where change is possible. It compares three main areas of strategic change – technical, cultural and political – against four areas of human resource activity, including structure, people, tasks and any informal organisational structure. The resulting twelve areas of the matrix are all considerations which may be leveraged in order to induce change. In practice, some will be more important than others and should be prioritised accordingly. A study of the cultural web greatly helps the process. The decision of how and when to implement change will depend on the style of leadership and the culture of the organisation.

If you track the performance of the organisation during the change process, possibly through profitability or share price, you will often discover that the performance will at first deteriorate. This process has been identified by Richard Whittington and others (1999) and is called the J-curve because during the change process the organisation's performance is likely to get worse before it gets better. This is understandable when you consider that systems need to be integrated and the organisation often undergoes a period of introversion rather than being customer-focused.

Taking it **FURTHER**

We have assumed in this text that organisational structure is modified according to the strategy that is to be implemented. Alfred Chandler (1962) and others have determined that in most cases organisations follow this process to best achieve the strategic implementation with the greatest efficiencies. However, it has also been identified that on occasions, strategy can be influenced by the structure of the organisation. For example, decentralised multidivisional organisations can provide a relatively simple platform for acquisitions or divestment of non-core or failing divisions, and decentralised organisations also tend towards diversified strategies. The key message is that an organisational structure should not determine the strategy just because it is convenient, but neither should the structure act as a restraint in implementing key strategies.

EXAMPLE QUESTIONS

This is a very broad area of study and so the questions can be very varied in nature. They may be specific multiple-choice or short-answer questions, or more likely subsections to other essay-based strategic evaluations. Links between structure, control and culture are common and if possible they should be evaluated in advance of your examination. Here are three example questions to test your knowledge and understanding:

1 *Which one of the following is not part of the 7-S framework?*

   (a) Supply chain.
   (b) Staff.
   (c) Skills.
   (d) Systems.

The wrong item is (a) supply chain. The others are constituent parts of the 7-S framework, and are useful to remember when developing a strategy. The value chain or supply chain would be evaluated under structure and systems.

2 *Critically debate the notion that organisational structure influences the culture of the organisation.*

This short-answer question is looking for an answer that discusses a number of structural types and the resulting cultures that occur. You might find it useful to use Charles Handy's (1993) cultural types and link them both to the structures that they represent and to different organisational examples. The key thread to your answer should be to identify that the more standardised the processes or manufacture, the more likely it is that there will be rules and regulations governing them, probably supervised by a hierarchy. A more creative organisation equates to fewer rules, a flatter structure and a wider range of networks and alliances. Under these conditions, the culture has to be strong and clearly defined.

3 *Using relevant academic model(s), critically evaluate the type(s) of strategic change that took place in Hewlett Packard under the leadership of Carly Fiorina.*

This type of question is loved by lecturers as there is so much that you could mention in your answer. It therefore needs a logical structure, so first identify what the major strategic changes are. These might include structural, cultural, market focus or even employee remuneration. Determine the reasoning behind the strategic changes and the likelihood of acceptance by the stakeholders (a stakeholder map might be useful!). Your answer may then include a force field analysis which clearly shows the pushing and restraining forces for each strategy. Evaluate each force and how Carly Fiorina tried to counter the restraining forces by effective communication, tighter control, and the use of change agents, threats and rewards, etc.

Textbook guide

JOHNSON, SCHOLES & WHITTINGTON: *Chapter 14*
LYNCH: *Chapters 16, 21 and 22*
THOMPSON & MARTIN: *Chapters 15, 16 and 17*

2.16	
strategic leadership issues	

Three corporate level strategic issues have been selected in this chapter in order to provide additional background material for your strategic studies, particularly with respect to the value chain, corporate vision and turn-around strategies.

Knowledge, innovation and organisational learning

The culture and structure of an organisation will have a direct impact on an organisation that wishes to develop and extend its competitive advantage through *knowledge management* and innovation.

Organisational knowledge is the product of both learning and experience; it is shared between employees and accumulated through processes and systems.

Nonaka and Takeuchi (1995) have identified two types of knowledge: *explicit* and *tacit knowledge*:

1   Explicit knowledge, which can be shared, stored and copied.

2   Tacit knowledge, which is based upon personal experience, is difficult to communicate and is developed through practice.

Clearly, an organisation can assist the transfer and storage of explicit knowledge by providing communication opportunities and information management systems and databases. These can be used by employees anywhere in the world in order to gain information which will help them to make decisions. This information will be useful in itself but not sufficient without the addition of tacit knowledge that the experienced employee brings. Tacit knowledge can only be transferred by socialisation in formal or informal settings. Together, explicit and tacit knowledge provide the organisation's intellectual capital. This can be demonstrated in many different forms, for example through:

- employee skills and experience
- brand image and reputation
- patents and designs
- financial management ability
- processes and procedures
- research and development skills
- customer relationships
- network alliances.

Consider all of these when evaluating an organisation's intrinsic value. They may be gained internally or developed in conjunction with an external source, such as through an alliance. They are difficult to measure but often make up the majority of any financial valuation if the company is likely to be purchased.

It is usually the tacit knowledge that delivers the real, sustainable competitive advantage. Many service organisations, such as consultancies and insurance brokers, rely predominantly on tacit knowledge in order to deliver creative and customised solutions to clients' problems.

Davenport and Prusak (1998) have identified six ways that organisations can help in knowledge creation:

1 By hiring experts such as consultants.

2 By setting up research centres in order to create knowledge (e.g. Honda's research institute).

3 By using teamwork to bring together a fusion of backgrounds and ideas.

4 By adapting to external pressures, thus encouraging change and development.

5 By introducing networks of informal communities of learning.

6 By acquiring or using another organisation's ideas.

Innovation is the process by which a creative idea is turned into a product or process and which may then be used to generate a competitive advantage.

An organisation's ability to *innovate* is difficult to quantify, except perhaps by counting the number of patent applications. Innovation is commonly linked to technological advances, although this does not need to be the case as many excellent ideas are simple modifications of existing technologies, or are 'discovered' through finding new uses for existing technologies. Consider, for example, a tough but light fabric that was originally developed for parachutes but is now also used for tents and cagoules, or using the mobile phone as a means to pay for items instead of using cash.

> **Note**
>
> Managing innovation and creativity in large organisations is often very difficult as the structural boundaries and task-orientated cultures often lack the flexibility and time that is required for the creative process. True creativity is often identified as being particularly relevant to small-to-medium enterprises (SMEs).

Innovation is not without risk, but if successful it can project a company into a leading market position. Indeed, in some highly competitive industries, there is a need to constantly innovate. For example, during a period of rapid growth in the printer market, Hewlett Packard were launching a new printer every six weeks. Admittedly, not all the products were significantly different from the previous ones, but each release served to keep their competitive edge and to keep the market fresh. There are two potential strategies for innovation, *market pull* and *technology push*:

1 **Market pull**. Satisfying the needs of the customer (usually determined by survey) by developing appropriate technology.

2 **Technology push**. The use of emergent scientific developments in ways that the customer may not have considered. Consider, for example, a market survey which asked consumers to list future enhancements to TVs – how many would have requested the development of a TV remote control?

If you are asked to comment on the innovative ability of an organisation, it is important to link these factors with the product portfolio and market analysis and ask the following questions:

- Has the organisation recently launched products or services that have a *first-mover advantage?*
- Is the company entering a market that has already been proven and can therefore build on the gains and developments of existing companies?
- Is the market unproven?
- Does the organisation have the capacity for rapid scale-up?
- Is there the potential for economies of scale and scope?
- Does the new technology comply with industry standards?
- Does the consumer need to be educated to appreciate the advantages of the product? Is the product complex? Will it need demonstrating?
- Are there potential rivals who may enter the market with much greater geographic reach and more resources?

The manner in which the organisation is structured and the culture is engendered also plays an important part in the ability of an organisation to be innovative. It may be useful to consider the following when analysing a company:

- Is there clarity of vision and top-down support for new initiatives?
- Are small teams of people working on project tasks?
- Is it a smaller, flatter organisation?
- Is there an informal structure, with few barriers between divisions?
- Is there a previous history of sponsored development throughout the company?

- Is there a learning organisation ethos, with multiple opportunities to share ideas within the company, the industry and elsewhere?
- Are there network links with external research establishments?

> *Take time to look at the relative pace of technological development within the industry and look for evidence of government sponsorship or alliances with research establishments, for example with universities. The quality of scientific education that is provided by the country is also an indicator of future potential. This may already have come to light through your PESTEL analysis.*

Governance and corporate social responsibility

Governance frameworks stipulate the priorities, processes and responsibilities of the organisation to the owners and to those whom the organisation serves. In the case of a public sector organisation, the primary stakeholders will include the government and the general public, and regular audits are undertaken in order to assess 'value for money'. In the case of a publicly quoted company, a non-executive body and the shareholders will be monitoring the actions of the executive and independent auditors will be checking the financial books. There are many laws and regulations relating to *corporate governance* and business practice, and while they differ from country to country, they are mainly concerned with honesty, fiscal openness, independence and the legal responsibilities of the executive. These are particularly valid when you consider the recent examples of corrupt accounting practice, as demonstrated by companies including Enron, WorldCom and Parmalat.

More specifically, corporate governance principles include checking:

- the organisation's financial statements for accuracy and transparency
- the internal controls and the independence of the organisation's auditors
- the resources that are made available to the directors
- the level of risk being taken
- the compensation arrangements of senior executives
- the process by which executives are nominated
- the processes to ensure transparency and openness with regard to share dealing and dividend policy.

The primary responsibility for the governance and success of an organisation lies with the governing body, which takes different forms in different parts of the world. In the UK and the USA, governance of the board is maintained by *non-executive directors* whose role is to act as an impartial steward on behalf of the shareholders, thus ensuring that the principal-agent model works effectively.

In other countries, a two-tier system operates which may involve shareholders or employees. This helps to ensure openness but does tend to slow decision-making. Recent scandals in the USA and the EU have shown that previous legislation was insufficient and has since been tightened, for example, with the Sarbanes-Oxley Act (2002) in the USA and the Higgs report (2003) in the UK.

Business ethics and *corporate social responsibility* (CSR) build on governance systems and are at the core of strategic leadership and corporate strategy.

Corporate social responsibility is the standard and manner in which an organisation undertakes its moral responsibilities to the wider society. It is the level of corporate citizenship demonstrated above the minimal requirements of governance and the law.

However, the relevance, importance and necessity of organisational involvement with corporate social responsibility is a matter of hot debate. The reason there is such controversy over this issue is not whether it is a good thing to be doing, but rather the degree to which organisations should engage in being a good corporate citizen. Should making profit and ensuring future viability for the shareholders be the overriding responsibility, or do organisations have other obligations to a wider range of stakeholders?

Clearly, there are many (if not most) situations where the situation is not black and white. For example, does a company engage in giving gifts to its major customers? When does this constitute poor business practice? What value might be placed on the gift before it became a bribe? What about gift-giving in cultures where it is normal and expected practice?

CSR differs from business ethics as business ethics is the ability to decide between right and wrong and is embodied in the standards and conduct of the organisation. With CSR, the organisation is considering its position of responsibility to the wider community.

The following list provides an insight into the CSR activities in which the organisation may be involved.

- **External aspects**

    - **Environmental issues** – Pollution and biodiversity, recycling, energy efficiency, packaging, etc.
    - **Product safety** – Electrical, fire hazard, small components, appropriate labelling, etc.
    - **Marketing strategies** – Advertising standards, ethical marketing techniques.
    - **Treatment of suppliers** – Prompt payment, partnership agreements, etc.
    - **Honesty** – Openness in business dealings, not using misleading information, avoidance of bribes.
    - **Human rights activities** – Child labour, union rights, poor conditions, etc.
    - **Charitable and community support activities** – Local community involvement.

- **Internal aspects**

    - **Employee welfare** – Medical care, working conditions, work/life balance, holiday entitlement, training and career development, health and safety, etc.
    - **Data protection** – Respecting private activities and intellectual property.
    - **Discrimination policy** – Equal opportunities and rights of employees.

Research has suggested that being a good corporate citizen may actually be beneficial to the business, both by improving the corporate image and enhancing shareholder value. This may be because the organisation is likely to be more aware of its workforce and environment and therefore the potential benefits and risks. Certainly, for companies whose leaders have embraced CSR as a core strategy, such as the Body Shop and Ben & Jerry's, it seems to have worked, although cynics might suggest that it is just a clever marketing tool, or at least a competitive differentiator. Most organisations have a section on their websites and in their annual reports detailing their CSR and ethical activities, which is known as 'social accounting' or 'the green bottom line'. However, you should be aware that this highly fashionable trend was also practised by Enron, some of whose board members have now been charged with a variety of crimes including conspiracy and insider trading.

> *Don't be tempted to take at full face value those organisations that are just paying lip-service to CSR. Look for signs that their CSR is fully incorporated into their core strategic planning.*

Strategies for failing industries

Not all organisations succeed at all times and even the most successful organisations need to undertake organisational renewal, particularly when minor strategic adjustments have made very little difference to the organisation's performance. Failure may be due to changes in the environment which have not been addressed, poor financial control which often leads to increased costs, a changing market or competitive situation, or possibly inappropriate corporate strategies.

Public service organisations and companies working within a protected environment, such as a nationalised industry or in a monopoly situation, can often continue to produce goods and services even though they may be highly inefficient. The recognition of this has led to a trend of privatisation and the increasing involvement of private companies in the running of previously nationalised organisations. However, unless the organisation is placed in a highly competitive situation, it is unlikely that it will perform as well as those that are succeeding within a competitive market.

When analysing a failing organisation, it is a great opportunity to put yourself in a strategic leadership position and decide what you would do under the circumstances. Start by looking at the financial position, particularly with regard to revenue generation and profitability. If the organisation is competing well in a growing market and the revenue streams are increasing but the profitability is low, price increases and/or cost reductions are clearly in order. However, if the income revenues have been stagnant or falling, it is time to look at the products and services and to realign your competitive strategies with the target market. In other words, you should ask if the organisation is 'stuck in the middle' (Porter's generic strategy) or undertaking a competitive strategy that is destined to fail (strategy clock). It could be that the products are insufficiently differentiated or possibly that the price is no longer competitive.

Under these circumstances, internally focused renewal strategies are most likely to be implemented and may be categorised as:

- **Consolidation, retrenchment and downsizing**: These look predominantly at the weaknesses of an organisation and in the short term aim to stabilise losses, increase revenue, improve value chain efficiency, rationalise the product line, dispose of fixed assets, re-evaluate sources of finance, re-evaluate return on investment and generally refocus efforts on the core business.
- **Turnaround.** This usually means that an organisation's survival is the motive for strategic change and more drastic measures are required.

The major costs to most organisations are those of labour costs and energy usage. Of the two, it is usually easier and quicker to make the biggest impact on labour costs by making redundancies. Shareholders often appreciate these announcements and this is reflected in the share price. However, if an organisation is downsizing and looking for voluntary redundancies, employees with experience and key skills may be quickly lost as they are the most employable.

A consolidation strategy might include a hiring freeze or a reduction on travel expenditure; a turnaround strategy might look for redundancies and possibly the closure of inefficient plants. When looking for cost reduction or income generation, the corporate strategist may consider outsourcing, or selling or divesting parts of the organisation that are not core to the primary business. For example, private contractors are often used to provide security, cleaning and catering services, and IBM sold their 'personal computing' division to Lenovo, in order to concentrate on their main-frame and consulting business.

Removing non-core parts of the organisation can provide multiple benefits when consolidating a failing business. Outsourcing offers the management 'breathing space' to maintain a customer base and contain costs while focusing on its core business. Selling parts of the organisation also removes a problem and enables focus elsewhere. The sale may be to existing management through a management buyout, to another company or to an investment company that sees the potential to asset strip, or to turn around the company with a short-term exit strategy such as stock flotation. Organisations should consider the following points before making a decision to divest:

- Is there potential growth in the current products?
- Can the current resources be more efficiently used elsewhere?
- Is there a market where competitive advantage may be gained?
- Is it failing due to a lack of investment?

- Would there be a direct or indirect impact elsewhere in the organisation if it was divested?
- Are there alternative uses for the assets?
- Is it likely to raise sufficient funds if it were to be divested?
- How would the stakeholders (including employees and customers) react?
- Will it be easy to find a buyer who is willing to pay an appropriate amount for the business?

Remember that divesting and other forms of cost-cutting are unlikely to turn around a failing organisation on their own. Refocusing on the target market segments and product and market development are also essential.

Taking it *FURTHER*

Organisations are now starting to use artificial intelligence systems which are computer programs which show some of the characteristics of learning and reasoning. More traditional uses for systems such as these include advanced chess games (Deep Blue), strategic logistics (as used in the Gulf war) and toy robots (e.g. Furby). More recently, advanced algorithms have been used as an approach to learning – you may have heard the terms 'data mining', 'machine vision', 'Bayesian and neural networks', 'fuzzy systems' and 'evolutionary computation'. These achieve learning by processing large amounts of known information or by looking for patterns in apparently random environments, and by providing conclusions based upon them. Systems such as these are being increasingly used for control, planning and scheduling, and will also have the ability to answer technical and consumer questions, read handwriting, use natural language and recognise faces. As yet, artificial intelligence doesn't offer 'comprehension', but you can expect that organisations will increasingly rely upon these sophisticated systems to provide much of the organisational knowledge, learning and decision-making in the future.

EXAMPLE QUESTIONS

If asked questions on leadership issues, you should attempt to make connections with all the relevant strategic frameworks but in particular with Ansoff's growth development matrix. Evidence of extra reading will definitely help you win extra marks, particularly if you can link your examples to the theory. Some example questions are listed below.

1 *Which of the following is not overseen by corporate governance procedures?*

  (a) *Fiscal transparency.*
  (b) *Levels of risk.*
  (c) *Recruitment of senior executives.*
  (d) *Data protection.*

The answer is (d). Data protection is covered by legislation other than governance law. The non-executive board (however it is structured) is not concerned with the routine activities required to run the organisation, but focuses on the other factors that could mask inappropriate agent behaviour.

2 *Using examples, debate the changing role of an organisational leader, highlighting how the role has been made more complex in the past 20 years.*

This question requires some thought and a logical structure to your answer. You might start by making a list of the major changes in technology and communication and highlighting the rapidly changing nature of many markets. Examine the trend of post-industrial organisations moving towards a knowledge and service base with an increasing emphasis on customer relationship management. Also consider the wider scope of organisational changes, with increasing drives for efficiency, knowledge and innovation management, CSR, stakeholder and alliance management. Figure 2.2 will be of help here.

3 *Critically discuss the assertion that a socially responsible attitude to doing business is increasingly important to an organisation's strategy and financial success.*

This question requires an answer that identifies the key benefits of CSR, in particular the reduction of risk due to enhanced social awareness, and the increasing benefits to the organisational image that being socially responsible might bring. You should detail examples, including the enhancement of employee welfare which benefits motivation and loyalty and therefore productivity, product safety, increasing customer satisfaction, energy conservation saving power bills, working in partnership with stakeholders to ensure support in strategy implementation, etc. You may also be awarded extra marks for mentioning that ethical investment funds are seeking to invest in socially responsible companies.

Textbook guide

JOHNSON, SCHOLES & WHITTINGTON: *Chapters 4, 6, 9 and 13*
LYNCH: *Chapters 10 and 11*
THOMPSON & MARTIN: *Chapters 2 and 14*

part three
study, writing and revision skills

3.0

introduction

The purpose of this section is to provide you with suggestions to help maximise your chance of examination success. A great many people claim in later life that they wish they had tried harder at school or university, and if given the opportunity again, many would now approach their learning in a more structured and motivated manner. Most readers of this Course Companion will have already studied for several years in higher education and this is likely to be your final year of undergraduate study, so you won't need me to remind you how important it is! It is certainly not too late to add to and improve your skills. Not only will this maximise your chance of success, but it may also help you to cope with the additional stresses of the final year. Importantly, the skills that you are introduced to in this section are lifetime skills – not only will they prepare you for lifelong learning, but they will also be very useful in the workplace.

You might like to consider these skills as a tool box, complete with a full set of learning tools. As with any new tool, in order to gain full advantage from its use you have to learn how to use it, when to use it, practise using it and to remember to maintain it! This is unlikely to happen without some effort on your part – the vast majority of people have to work very hard to make things look easy. Take, for example, someone giving a speech without notes, perhaps even your lecturer! They may have previously written down the key themes of what they intend to say, structured their talk in a logical manner and memorised the key points, all amounting to hours of preparation for a 'simple' no-notes talk!

Note

Some tools are more suited to some tasks than others and often they can be used together, for example, memory techniques with time management skills. All will be useful in the workplace and their transferability to the workplace is summarised at the end of each chapter.

3.1

reflective learning

This section will show you how to:

- use reflection as a self-development tool
- use reflection as part of a cycle of learning
- learn effectively.

You will have already noticed that learning at university is very different from studying at school; the emphasis is much more on the individual student's own motivation to study. The tutors act predominantly as signposts, showing you what you need to learn by teaching the core themes of the subject, but the background reading and gaining a deeper understanding of the subject area is your responsibility. The emphasis should not be on how you are taught; it is the focused effort that you put into understanding and remembering. This is not easy but it does become second nature and, with practice, it will give you a great deal of satisfaction. But first you have to *train your brain*!

Using reflection as a self-development tool

In order to be able to undertake this effectively you should reflect on your own abilities and experiences. You need to identify any weaknesses that you need to correct and strengths that you need to maximise. The following provides a hint of some of the areas that you might consider as a start to the reflective process:

1 What is your motivation for doing your course?

2 Why do you want to do well?

3 What is the next step after you graduate?

4 What subjects do you most enjoy, and why?

5   Are you struggling with the workload, and why?

6   What forms of assessment do you most enjoy, and why?

7   Is anything stopping your learning? For example:

    (a)   lack of motivation

    (b)   anxiety (e.g. through homesickness)

    (c)   inappropriate environment

    (d)   previous bad learning experience.

8   Why do you do better in some subjects than others?

9   Do you feel that your friends are coping better than you? Is there anything you can learn from them?

10   Which style of tutoring do you most like, and why?

You can evaluate these and other questions in a more formal manner, for example, by using self-evaluation questionnaires or progress sheets – your academic office, student support services or library may be able to provide these. But even without these aids, you can start the process by jotting down notes. For example, you may find the subject of business finance more difficult than human resources; think about why this may be. When you start to break down to the subject detail, you might identify that a particular area of mathematics is limiting your understanding, or conversely in human resources that you enjoy the experience of working in groups.

Note

It is normal to find some subjects harder than others; but this does provide the opportunity to put a greater emphasis on the weaker subjects. Don't assume that your friends are finding everything easy; often they will be struggling with other subjects, or perhaps they are working harder and more effectively than you, even if they don't admit it!

In order to benefit from this reflection, you need to act on your findings, for example, a weakness in mathematics may be resolved by focused effort, working with friends or personal tuition. Similarly, when deconstructing your human resources group work experiences, you will find out what your strengths are, such as team leadership, project management or presentation skills. Think of how you can utilise these skills in other areas.

Using reflection as part of a cycle of learning

David Kolb (1984) recognised the importance of reflection and integrated it into a learning cycle which contains four sequential elements:

1. **Active experimentation.** You learn through the practice of doing, making mistakes and learning from them.

2. **Concrete experiences.** Definitive experience has now been gained, and the feelings that come out of this are useful in developing future learning.

3. **Reflective observation.** Reflection on previous learning experience is very important at this stage as it provides the basis for taking additional action.

4. **Abstract conceptualisation.** This is where the creation of new concepts is undertaken. The reflection on previous experience provides a springboard for new theories to be considered and tested, leading you back to active experimentation.

Note the importance of experimenting and making mistakes when learning. Use difficulties and questions as signals for to you to actively engage in the learning process. Solving problems provides a sense of achievement and purpose which in itself is a motivational tool to encourage further active learning.

Think about an occasion when you did not understand a concept. How did you overcome this hurdle? Reflect on the lessons learned. Could you use the same means in the future?

Learning effectively

Hard work is also a prerequisite for most subjects but don't confuse long hours of hard work with effective working – working efficiently results in less hours better spent. Efficient working requires focused effort or *active learning*. The following tips should be followed to ensure that your learning is as active, efficient and effective as possible.

Learning style

- Always make notes when reading, as it focuses the mind and helps memory retention, and you can also later review it with ease.
- You will work more effectively in short intense spells rather than in long sessions.
- Summarise things in your own words, once you have understood the basis of the argument.
- Work with others when appropriate.
- Work in an uninterrupted environment. Switch off your phone, email and web messenger.

Using information

- Selectively read a wide range of materials, rather than one book in detail.
- Ask yourself questions and find the answers.
- Reproduce information in a different format, perhaps as a diagram or mind-map.
- Use your notes to highlight the key points rather than the detail.

Broadening your horizons

- Identify overlapping and connecting subject areas.
- Relate theory to current news articles.
- Look for examples to illustrate theory.
- Be critical when reviewing data or theory.

Note

The most important step in learning is to start making notes. Do not put things off by convincing yourself that before you can work well, you need the pressure of an imminent deadline. This may be true but it is also an excuse for inaction. Manage your time wisely by creating your own achievable targets which are set before the final deadline.

Links to transferable skills

Self-analysis and reflection are key skills that will help you to develop as a person throughout your career. A proactive employer will encourage you to undertake reflection and will help you to achieve this with performance evaluations and feedback from other colleagues. Seeing yourself as others see you can be a liberating experience, once you have got over your surprise! This process may at first be a little frightening, but until you recognise what your strengths and weaknesses are, you cannot hope to focus your development as a person. Use the information gained from the exercise and turn it to your advantage.

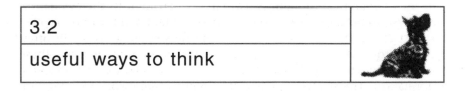

3.2	
useful ways to think	

This section will show you how to use:

- analytical thinking
- critical thinking
- lateral thinking.

We take thinking for granted but in reality there are many different ways that people can approach the same problem. When working in groups, have you noticed how some people always seem to have the good ideas that no one else has thought of? Or you may have wondered why some people are good at cryptic crossword puzzles and others do not understand the questions, or often even the answers? This is often nothing to do with intelligence or even knowledge, but merely a way of thinking. This section will introduce just three types of thinking, all of which are complementary to each other but each is an important skill which will help you with your studies and future careers.

Thinking analytically

This form of thinking is vital in the evaluation of any information. You might like to consider this form of thinking as similar to scientific evaluation as it requires similar thought processes:

- A methodical approach to breaking down problems or scenarios into their constituent parts.
- An understanding of the logic and structure of the information.
- The ability to identify cause-and-effect patterns.
- An unbiased perspective.
- Checking the validity of the conclusions against the supporting evidence.
- Looking for discrepancies between the information and other sources, including a comparison against your knowledge.
- Identifying similarities or differences within complex information.

The use of analytical thought is particularly pertinent in the evaluation or analysis of business case studies or financial tables, but can be applied to most circumstances. In the case of business strategy, you will often be asked to analyse a case study using appropriate frameworks – these are your analytical tools which help you to categorise and evaluate information. The strategic tools will provide a framework to categorise information and allow it to be evaluated further, looking for trends, similarities, inconsistencies and differences. Details on how to use these strategic tools may be found in the appropriate section.

Ensure that you only use information that is supported by reasonable evidence, preferably from a reliable source, such as textbooks or journals. These have been checked for academic rigour and the information that is presented will be supported by previous studies.

Thinking critically

Have you ever wondered why the same news story is often written from a different perspective depending on the newspaper or form of media? Taking the viewpoint of just one author with their own sources of information, aims and objectives often does not give a full and accurate representation of the true story. This is because each journalist presents the article from their own viewpoint, or at least that of their editor and readers. So in order to get a true representation of the facts, you should read a variety of reports, preferably comparing these with other news services, such as TV and radio. This underlines the importance of critical thinking. Critical writing is discussed later in your Course Companion.

Critical thinking requires understanding and the ability to analyse and internally debate the strengths and weaknesses of an argument based on the available evidence.

The skill of looking at information and critically evaluating it is an essential tool. You should never accept information at 'face value'; always judge whether it is valid and supportable by comparing it with other sources of information.

> **Note**
>
> This may sound obvious, but unfortunately people often do not think critically when the information is within the framework of their existing perceptions. Or, in other words, people do not critically consider data or a piece of information if it seems to be reasonable, presented in a professional manner or delivered with authority.

The following checklist will help to ensure that you are thinking in a critical way:

- Identify the main points and conclusions that are being made.
- Test the logic of the argument. Does one point lead to another?
- Are there other conclusions that can be made?
- Question if you have all the relevant information.
- Is the information from a reliable and unbiased source?
- Have stereotypes been used to support an argument?
- What are the assumptions that are made? Are they reasonable?
- Have false analogies (similarities) been made?
- Question the accuracy, date, sample size and validity of data or statistics that are being presented.
- Does the evidence fully support the conclusions?
- Has emotive language been used?
- Have some aspects been given less prominence than they deserve?
- What has been left out? Is this significant?

The information that is not displayed is often more revealing than that which is, for example, bold letters on a can of fizzy drink may claim the contents have less than 0.1% fat. For marketing reasons, the manufacturer does not make an equally prominent reference to the high sugar content!

Note

Students are often tempted to get most of their information from organisation websites. These sites, however, are more akin to an electronic marketing brochure for the organisation and often make enthusiastic and possibly exaggerated claims about their products and services. While you can expect it to be factual, much of it will also be biased and misrepresented. Have you have ever found any company literature claiming that they have the second best product in the market?

In business, financial figures are often 'favourably' manipulated in order to present a successful financial year. For example, large expenditures may be adjusted to fall into the following financial year to avoid the loss appearing at a detrimental time. Most of these activities are within the financial regulations but they also serve to artificially support share prices and enhance the perception of the consumer. For example, a well-known multinational company submits its accounts under different country jurisdictions depending on how positive the accounts look with each; on one occasion, this turned what could have been shown as a large loss into a small profit.

When reading business reports, look for information that may be based on an assumption or error and which, upon repeated telling, quickly becomes a 'fact' in the same way that Chinese whispers work. Try to find the original source of the information. It may not be attributed to a reliable source, it may be taken out of context, or it may have been exaggerated. Also read between the lines of what is being said or perhaps not being said. Most importantly, look for opposing opinions so that you can make your own judgement of the facts.

Note

You will even find that some editorials are written by journalists who have been provided with 'approved' information and paid directly by the company that they are reviewing. This may then be 'dressed up' as investigative journalism.

Even when appropriate research has been undertaken, it will be subject to some bias and this may be highlighted by the researcher. However, for marketing purposes, you can often get the answer you want by surveying a suitable pre-selected sample or by asking a leading question or by reviewing data in a particular way. Cosmetics companies are renowned for making bold claims about their 'skin regenerating' creams, for example, '67% claimed to have seen an improvement in their skin tone after two weeks of use'. Look at the small print. These claims are often based on a very small number of carefully selected volunteers, the research is undertaken by the company itself and does not represent critical independent evidence.

> **Note**
>
> Even business consultants can be keen to produce a report that is not too dissimilar from one that was produced on a previous occasion. If they are too controversial, they may not be taken seriously and may not be considered for future contracts!

Thinking laterally

Lateral thinking is a term that was first coined by Edward de Bono (1967) as a means to describe a way in which perceptions can be changed. It is particularly powerful when there is a need to think creatively and innovatively. Comedians are usually very good lateral thinkers as they look at mundane activities from a different perspective and make us laugh. Lateral thinking is a powerful thinking tool to practise, especially when there are intractable problems which can't be solved by other means and must therefore be worked around.

> **Note**
>
> Children are also natural lateral thinkers because at an early stage of development they haven't experienced an educational system (which is more aligned to problem-solving and analytical thought), and so they will often look at things from a different perspective and say amusing things or find 'unusual' ways of completing a simple task.

Business strategies are often by nature logical and evidence-based. However, some of the most successful companies have taken a traditional product, thought about it laterally and re-launched it to great success. Take, for example, the computer mouse. Clearly, a PC mouse is inappropriate for laptop use and this has spurred a whole range of imaginative alternatives such as tracker balls (upside down mouse), keyboard nipples, sensor mats, smaller optical mice, styluses, touch screens, etc., all of which achieve the same objective of moving a cursor on a screen.

Note

It often happens that organisations can get too close to their products and processes and it needs an outsider, such as a consultant, to think laterally and to take a fresh look at complex problems, perhaps by 'going back to basics'.

As a strategy student, you should try to think 'out of the box' and develop suggestions based on different patterns of thinking. These may at first appear unconventional but some could eventually provide a strategic solution. You might find techniques such as brainstorming useful to stimulate this activity. You can practise lateral thinking at any time and with any example. Be as bizarre and strange as you like with your ideas, as some may actually be possible. Take, for example, a company that is finding it hard to find a reliable supplier to regularly deliver an important component on time. The 'knee-jerk' reaction might be to financially penalise the supplier. However, by applying some lateral thought, you might generate the following alternative possibilities or, using Edward de Bono's term, 'provocations' (de Bono, 1967):

- Acquire the supplier.
- Provide facilities for the supplier in your manufacturing facility.
- Build a 'buffer stock' at the supplier's expense.
- Arrange your own collection from the supplier's warehouse.
- Integrate logistics software systems.
- Arrange for the component to be manufactured under licence elsewhere.
- Move the manufacturing facility closer to the supplier.
- Re-engineer the product so that the component is no longer required.
- Sell the product division to another company – possibly even the supplier.
- Change manufacturing schedules to accommodate batch deliveries.
- Make the component in-house.
- Purchase and cannibalise other products to obtain the component.

Note

Many of these suggestions may appear extreme and impractical, but sometimes, with modification, they can provide a solution to a problem. For example, some car manufacturers are now renting space to key suppliers within their factory complex in order to provide tighter control over quality, supply and future development.

Links to transferable skills

There are obvious connections here with skills that are highly desirable in the workplace. People with the ability to think analytically or critically are most likely to find work in numerical or complex situations where clear logical thought and perhaps attention to detail is of benefit. Lateral thinkers will soon be recognised as an important contributor, particularly in teams where the creative aim is problem-solving or design. But whatever the role, you will find all forms of thinking will help to provide robust decision-making and help to protect against 'spin' and manipulation.

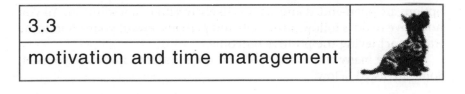

3.3
motivation and time management

This section will show you how to:

- motivate yourself to study
- manage your time wisely
- combat stress.

As you will have discovered, studying at university brings a whole range of new challenges. There are many temptations out there: you may be living away from home, and you will have new friends and interests, all of which are exciting and important to develop but they often tend to detract from your studies. Perhaps for the first time, you need to manage your own time. This will take some independent resolve, planning and motivation.

Motivating yourself to study

Finding time to fit in your study is actually relatively easy. Unfortunately, the tendency is to find something else to do which is more interesting or requires less effort! Others can set you targets or deadlines and even provide encouragement, but it is only you who can motivate yourself. As a quick check on your level of motivation, what would you do if you do not understand something in your lecture?

- Hope that during the next few teaching sessions things will become clearer?
- Try to remember to ask your friend or tutor about it next time you see them?
- Make a mental note to go to the library and get a book on the subject?
- Have a quick look on the internet, where you might be distracted by something else you find?
- Plan some time between teaching sessions to read your textbook, and if you still can't understand, make an appointment to see your tutor?

Hopefully, you have selected the final option as the most appropriate course of action. This is because there is a defined time allocated in the near future, there is a course of action and a follow-up plan. The other options are open-ended and are less likely to end in a resolution. All you now have to do is follow it through and perhaps reward yourself in some way for achieving the positive outcome.

There are many things that you can do in order to motivate yourself. Some are listed below:

- Remind yourself why you chose to study and what you hope to achieve. This might include

    - personal satisfaction
    - a first step to a chosen career
    - making new friends
    - learning more about a subject that interests you
    - broadening your horizons.

- Consider the consequences of failure.
- Break down large tasks into 'bite-sized' smaller and more achievable goals.
- Start working on the task!
- Celebrate by giving yourself small rewards, even if it is the evening off!
- Remind yourself of all your positive achievements; learn from but do not dwell on the less positive occasions.
- Surround yourself with like-minded positive people; don't let others drag you down.
- When you have succeeded, set yourself higher goals – anything is possible.

Keep focused and manage your time wisely; in this way, you will still have time both to work and play hard.

Managing your time wisely

Your formal teaching will often account for only a small fraction of the week. The rest, however, is not free time. It is time provided for independent study, although admittedly you can use it as you please.

> **Note**
>
> Independent study should include activities such as enhancing your notes, catching up with the recommended reading, improving your understanding, researching, preparing for lectures and seminars, writing assignments, etc.

Here are some hints to optimise your time and to help you to plan effectively:

1 Keep a detailed calendar of all the set (e.g. lecture) and flexible activities (e.g. self-study); many of these will be related to your 'to-do' or task list.

2 Make, prioritise and regularly update the task list.

3 Prioritise the least attractive tasks first; everything else is easy after that!

4 Utilise waiting time/dead time effectively. Read, plan or revise when waiting or travelling.

5 Set aside time for yourself – with no interruptions, just to think.

6 Plan well ahead so that there are no surprises.

7 Plan your independent study according to time patterns that most suit you.

8 Reward yourself whenever you complete tasks.

The first thing you need to do is to keep a detailed calendar of teaching and other formal activities. Using this as a template, you can identify the remaining times each week when you can spend time studying. You might find you have days that are completely clear of teaching or several hours between sessions that can usefully be used – the choice is obviously yours, so long as it is adequate to cover your workload and you stick to it! Some students prefer short bursts of intense work in complete solitude in order to study, and others work all night and sleep the next morning. Adjust your calendar to suit your learning style. Any remaining time is for relaxation and pleasure – your reward for the hard work.

> *Nearer examination time, consider allocating all spare slots in your calendar to self-study, even to the extent of giving up or reducing your paid employment.*

It is a good idea to create a to-do list of all the things that you have to do each week. These should be prioritised according to the relative urgency and importance of the task. For example, recommended reading can sometimes be less highly prioritised so long as it is not in preparation for a lecture or seminar, but don't keep putting it off! Large projects need to be subdivided into smaller, achievable tasks. Do this as soon as possible so you know the scale of what is required and can organise resources, such as reserving textbooks or arranging appointments well in advance.

> *Keep the to-do list with you at all times so that you can update it. Accept that some days it will grow rather than reduce in length! Also leave some extra time each week for urgent and unforeseen tasks – these will occur from time to time.*

If you are undertaking a large research project or dissertation, draw a timeline or use a Gantt chart and annotate it with milestone activities to ensure that you have time to complete it. Calculating that you have to write 10,000 words, which equates to about one week's writing, does not represent the hundreds of hours of research and reading that needs to be done before the writing starts. With your calendar, identify the fixed activities, including the teaching and holidays, and spread out the other activities equally over the timeline, leaving some 'buffer time' at the end for emergencies. Estimate the number of hours you are likely to need to spend on each activity and proportion the hours accordingly. You may find it easier to start from the deadline date and work backwards to the current date. Figure 3.1 shows how a timeline can be used. Ideally, it should be as detailed as possible, with all your major and

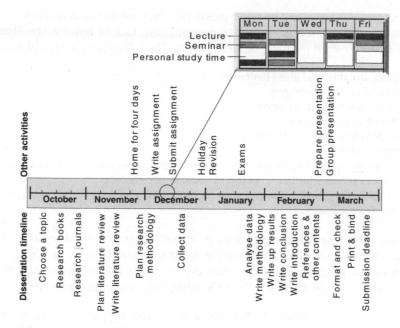

Figure 3.1   Example timeline

minor projects and personal activities. Note how the large dissertation project dovetails with the other activities.

Combating stress

One of the useful side-effects of effective time management is the feeling that you are in control. You may be busy and struggling to fit everything in but at least you know what you have to do, how long you have to do it and that, if you stick to your plan, you will achieve it. Those not keeping a close track on their 'to-do' tasks will either be blissfully unaware of the extent of what they are missing or highly stressed and feeling out of control with the enormity of the workload.

> **Note**
>
> This does not mean that stress is a bad thing. A small amount of stress can often help motivate you and focus the mind on the task. However, when it starts to affect your efficiency, then it is too much.

Stress can also be caused by other personal issues outside your control, such as relationships, troubles with accommodation, lack of money, etc. Stress can manifest itself in many different ways. The following are typical signs:

- being irritable and short-tempered
- having difficulty sleeping
- frequently getting hot and flushed
- having panic attacks
- having difficulty concentrating
- eating irregularly
- 'relaxing' by drinking or smoking. These might make you feel better but your body is actually further stressed by alcohol and nicotine
- exhibiting irrational behaviour such as tearing up your notes or absenting yourself from lectures.

If you recognise these symptoms, it is likely that you need to take control both of your tasks and lifestyle. Planning and managing your time is perhaps the most important means to combat the feeling of helplessness, but you can also take the following steps to reduce anxiety:

- Plan to sleep for at least eight hours, and rest your body and brain for at least 30 minutes before going to bed.
- Take regular exercise and breaks in what you are doing, even if it is just a walk down the road. This is not wasted time, as you can still think!
- If you are struggling with a problem, leave it and come back to it later. It is surprising how easily it is resolved with a fresh look.
- Eat healthily and regularly, and reduce alcohol and tobacco consumption.
- Re-assess your priorities: are things getting out of proportion? What is really important to you?
- Are you trying to be too much of a perfectionist?
- Take up a relaxation class, such as yoga or meditation, and practise this at home.

Links to transferable skills

Time-keeping and stress management are both soft skills that are vital in both your personal and professional life. In the workplace, courses on these subjects are very popular! Your first encounter with time management outside university may be an interviewer asking you for examples of previous project management, as they want to be assured that you can manage your time effectively. In the workplace, stresses caused by demands on your time are likely to be even higher, so university is a good place to lay the foundations of planning your lifestyle. No one else can do it for you!

3.4

speed reading

This section will show you how to:

- read selectively
- improve your concentration
- improve the speed that you read.

Given the enormous amount of material that you need to be reading, and not just for business strategy, selective reading, improving your concentration and reading at speed are certainly skills worth developing.

Reading selectively

It is unlikely that you will be able to read all the recommended papers and textbooks, even for business strategy, let alone for all your subjects. But this does not mean that you do not attempt to read these sources of information. As with most things in life, you will have to prioritise and use your time wisely. The following list provides ten tips to help you to optimise your time when reading the recommended texts.

1 Read all 'essential texts' and selectively scan other recommended reading.

2 Make full use of the summaries and abstracts in books and journals.

3 Work from up-to-date textbooks and research reviews that summarise current activities.

4 Skip paragraphs where there is significant factual detail, looking instead for the conclusion.

5 Use indexes, contents lists and subheadings to select relevant material.

6 Divide all the recommended reading between you and your trusted friends. Make and swap notes with each other.

7 Diagrams often say more than pages of text. If they are present, you can study these and review only the topics that need clarification.

8 Always make notes or highlight important phrases when reading as it engages the mind.

9 Improve your levels of concentration.

10 Practise speed reading.

Improving your concentration

Do you find yourself re-reading the same paragraph several times and yet you still do not remember a word? This is quite normal. The brain needs to take a frequent rest in order to absorb the information that it has to receive, which is why you should plan a short break typically every 30 minutes. You don't in fact stop concentrating but your mind will have decided to concentrate on something else! Tony Buzan (2006) has identified seven reasons which lead to poor concentration when reading:

1 **Vocabulary difficulties.** If you come across a word that is new to you, you have to think about it and perhaps look it up. This breaks the flow of incoming information and therefore disrupts your concentration.

2 **Conceptual difficulties.** If you are struggling to grasp the concepts, this will again distract you from absorbing information. Try to grasp the basics before delving deeper.

3 **Inappropriate reading speed.** The brain requires a fast input to work efficiently and will wander if the input is too slow. Try reading faster (see improving the speed that you read).

4 **Poor focus.** With other important tasks to do, it is sometimes difficult to concentrate on something else. Try to improve your focus with mind-mapping techniques (see later in this Course Companion).

5 **Poor organisation.** Make sure that you are in a suitable environment without distraction and have everything to hand.

6 **Lack of interest.** This is often linked to poor engagement due to other priorities, complexity of the document or a lack of motivation.

7 **Lack of motivation.** Understand why it is important to read the text, look for the relationship between your aims and that of the subject.

> **Note**
>
> Writing notes as you read helps to improve concentration as you are using different thought processes when you combine reading with the act of writing. You are also thinking about and reviewing the information as you write, giving time for the brain to recover. A useful 'spin-off' is that afterwards you can also review the key points without having to read the text again!

Improving the speed that you read

Unlike reading a novel, you have to be ruthless when reading large volumes of academic reference text. If you practise speed reading, you will not be reading every word. You will be recognising groups of words or even the shape of the words due to the letters they contain, and your brain will make assumptions and fill in the gaps without losing information. Reading at speed discourages the eye from wandering and 'back-reading' or re-reading the same words or sentence again, all of which takes time! To help you with your speed reading, you will find it useful to develop both scanning and skimming techniques.

Scanning is used when you are looking for specific words or information.

Skimming gains an overview of the information in order to get an impression of the content.

> *Depending on the material that you have to read, you may need to vary your reading speed. For example, detailed research papers containing complex arguments and vocabulary will need to be read in more detail than those of a case study where the writing style is that of a narrative. Nevertheless, skim reading to get an overall impression is always useful before you read sections in detail.*

Below is a list of hints adapted from Tony Buzan's (2006) work to help you to speed up your reading while maintaining your concentration and understanding.

- Ensure that you are sitting upright and comfortably, that the text is well lit and approximately 50 cm from your eyes. This distance will ensure that you have the correct field of vision to be able to speed read.
- Preview the content from an abstract or contents list before starting to read.
- If relevant, scan the text for specific words or information.
- Skim read documents, varying the pattern but never reading every word, for example:

  - read alternate lines
  - some paragraphs can be scanned diagonally while still absorbing the content
  - skim read some lines backwards, as your brain will still work it out!

- Quickly track with a pointer either along a line or down the side of the page – this hand-to-eye coordination helps to focus the activity and maintain your rhythm.
- Keep your eyes moving quickly.
- Take regular breaks if you feel you are losing concentration.
- Summarise the content with notes or draw a mind-map as soon as you have finished your session.
- Practise with different reading materials – you will get faster.

Note

When practised, speed reading actually enhances the content recall better than a slow reader. It … goes…. show …. don't need …. the words!

Links to transferable skills

Throughout your career and personal life, you will be reading. If you can read at twice the speed, imagine how many hours you can gain for yourself, or how much extra work you can get through. This is a vital skill that will save you significant time in which you can do other things. However, if you are ever in the position to ask for a report to be written, insist that there is a concise abstract and conclusion. The content is after all more important than the number of words, even if you can read twice as fast as everyone else!

3.5

memory techniques

This section will show you how to:

- optimise the memory process
- create and use mnemonics and memory aids
- stimulate creativity and aid memory through the use of mind-maps.

Your memory is a phenomenal thing. Even though you may think that it fails you when you can't remember something, you don't notice the continuous stream of occasions when it is working! During sleep, the brain filters and sorts what is important and what is not, and bases this 'decision' on whether the information has been recently used. It is therefore important to optimise your memory by 'revisiting' all the knowledge you have absorbed.

Optimising the memory process

Your brain consists of two hemispheres: the left and right brain.

- The left hemisphere (logical thinking) handles sequencing, words, numbers, reasoning, language, listing and similar activities.
- The right hemisphere (gestalt thinking) handles colour, faces, shapes, music, metaphor, imagination, special relationships, day dreaming, emotion and similar activities.

These sides of the brain are well connected and work closely together. Indeed, if there is physical damage, the opposite hemisphere can take over most of the tasks of the other hemisphere. Most activities use both sides of the brain, for example, when you watch someone singing, the left hemisphere recognises the lyrics and the name of the singer, the right hemisphere the tune and the face of the singer.

Note

Some people may use one hemisphere more than the other, for example, artistic people might be more right-brained, and mathematicians more left-brained. But research shows that both sides are required for creative and academic success.

In order to optimise your memory, you should combine activities from both sides of the brain by linking additional senses and preferably attaching some emotion to the process. Many people have experienced hearing some music, or smelling a particular smell which has immediately 'transported' them back to when they first experienced it, perhaps evoking emotion in the process. This is why connecting facts with emotions, patterns, colours, setting something to music or even writing it down will all help memory.

The memory process occurs in four stages:

1   Input of information.

2   Retaining information in the short-term memory (it doesn't stay here long!).

3   Revisiting it and encoding it so it can be stored in the main memory.

4   Recalling it when required – the more times it is recalled, the better the memory.

The third step is probably the most important stage as the encoding process indexes, files and stores the memory. You have to work a little at this stage, but with practice this will become semi-automatic. Grouping similar things together or seeing a pattern on a page will greatly aid the encoding process and this is the underlying principle of mnemonics and mind-maps.

Creating and using mnemonics and memory aids

There are many ways to encode information but they all include linking to another sense, to the opposite side of the brain or with a physical process.

> **Note**
>
> It has been calculated by Herbert Simon (1974) that we can only hold five pieces of information in our short-term memory, such as phone numbers or names, and these are likely to be lost after a few minutes unless they are reviewed and encoded in some way.

Below is a list of some suggestions and examples to help you encode information. For them to be truly effective, however, you should create your own versions:

- Order things alphabetically, colour code and count the number in each list.
- Play with and create pictures from words (e.g. change agent = secret agent). Conjure up a picture of a suitably shifty person with overcoat, hat and sunglasses wandering around an organisation persuading people to change their clothes!
- Group similar items together (e.g. Porter's five forces):
  - Power (buyer and supplier)
  - Threat (substitutes, new entrants)
  - Competitors.

- Place the words or phrases in an ordered hierarchy of importance (e.g. means of external development with increasing commitment):
  - exporting and subcontracting
  - franchising and strategic alliances
  - joint ventures and consortia
  - merger and acquisition.

- Arrange the words into a pattern and see what the pattern resembles (e.g. a star, a face, a hand, a house, etc.).
- Reword things so that they start with the same letter (e.g. the 7-S framework).
- Set words or phrases to a favourite tune (you know how good you are at remembering lyrics!).
- Arrange the information into an acronym so that the first letters spell a word (e.g. PESTEL).
- Create a sentence from the first letters of each piece of information or even whole words (e.g. Yip's globalisation drivers: Government, Competitor, Economic, and Marketing – 'Governments compete in economic markets').
- Identify key words and use these as memory triggers for the rest of the information.
- Connect each piece of information through a story – the more ridiculous the story, the more memorable it will be.
- What do the words sound like, or rhyme with, or remind you of? (For example, the three types of control system (feed-forward, feed-back and concurrent) are similar to the fast forward, rewind and play on a DVD recorder.)
- Use mind-maps.

Mind-maps

Mind-maps were brought to the world's attention by Tony Buzan (1993), the same author that popularised the concepts of memory training and speed reading. The technique can be used for:

1 Lecture note-taking.

2 Taking minutes of meetings.

3 Summarising your ideas or thoughts.

4 Brainstorming new ideas.

5 Forming a draft structure (e.g. an essay or presentation).

6 Looking for connections between disparate subjects.

7 Problem-solving.

8 Giving presentations and speeches.

9 Overcoming writer's block.

10 Aiding memory.

The mind-map is a multidimensional mnemonic, combining aspects of the left and right brain in order to enhance memory and creative function. The use of groups, hierarchies, sequences, patterns, colour and pictures can be included in your mind-map, thereby maximising the opportunity for learning. There are several rules to follow when constructing a mind-map. The following are adapted from Tony Buzan's (1993) work:

- Start with an image, problem, subject or theory in the centre of your page.
- Group related subjects or words together around this, preferably in a hierarchy.
- Note that the words should be on lines and each line should be connected to other lines.
- words should be in 'units' with one word per line, allowing each word to have 'free hooks' which give more freedom and flexibility.
- Use colours and pictures to enhance memory, delight the eye and stimulate the right hemisphere.
- Remember that the mind should be left as 'free' as possible. You will probably think of ideas and connections faster than you can write.

Constructing a mind-map is best demonstrated by an example. Figure 3.2 shows a mind-map which is the result of approximately ten minutes of brainstorming the attributes of paper.

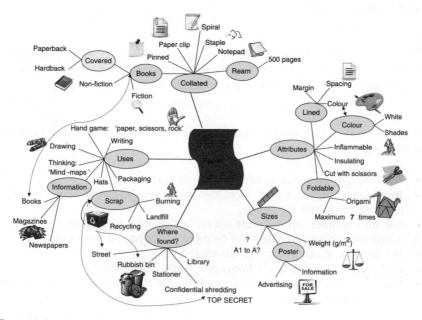

Figure 3.2   A mind-map using paper as a topic

This is a deliberately simple example, but the same principles work for any topic you choose. If you try this exercise, it is most likely to result in a different map, with different groupings, hierarchies and titles. It is also probable that it will be more complete, and include things I have not thought of. This doesn't matter, and in fact it is to be welcomed. The purpose is to stimulate thought, aid memory and to find connections (in this case, I have identified these with dotted arrows). It is surprising when you are brainstorming how you can seemingly go off at tangents (in this case into advertising, publishing and waste disposal!). Additionally, I have come across a gap in my knowledge – even on the 'simple' subject of paper! I have annotated this with a question mark and have since looked up the answer – if you are interested, paper comes in A1 to A10 sizes!

You could now use your mind-map as a memory exercise where you could identify the main subgroups, of which (in my case) there are five, and from then on fill in the gaps according to how your mind-map looks. You might remember having drawn flames, for example, which in turn may stimulate memories of other attributes, such as landfill sites and waste recycling.

Apart from being a useful aid to memory, mind-maps are an excellent way to make notes in lectures and meetings. After the lecture, redraw the mind-map as it may look cluttered. The re-writing process also reinforces the themes and structure in your memory.

Apart from being enjoyable to do, here are some more advantages of the technique:

- The centre or core topic is more clearly defined.
- The relative importance of each idea is clearly indicated. More important ideas will be nearer the centre.
- The links between key concepts will be immediately recognised.
- Information recall and review will be more effective and more rapid.
- The addition of new information is easy.
- Each map will look different from other maps, aiding recall.
- The open-ended nature of the map will enable the brain to identify new relationships far more readily.

Mind-maps are also useful in overcoming 'mental blocks', which is why they are used in creative thinking and brainstorming sessions in workplaces such as advertising agencies. Bizarre and amusing connections can be made which would probably not be associated with a more analytical process. Also use a mind-map to start the thought process when approaching an essay or examination answer, as it quickly stimulates thought and relationships and the result is a draft structure!

Links to transferable skills

Memory skills are clearly highly desirable in the workplace. Many people that you see giving speeches and lectures without notes, or even those who seem to have the capacity to always remember names, will be using techniques such as these. It is well worth practising them at every opportunity, as you will then be able to spend a lifetime using them to your advantage.

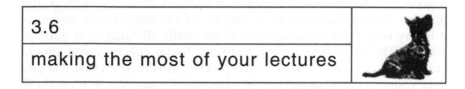

3.6	
making the most of your lectures	

This section will show you how to:

- optimise your learning before, during and after a lecture
- become an active rather than a passive learner
- make the best use of your lecture's learning outcomes
- take effective notes in lectures.

Optimising your learning

A lecturer is unable to deliver everything you need to know on the subject in less than one hour, so in order to optimise your time, you need to prepare and afterwards reflect upon and read around the subject. To help you in this process, you will have been given a reading list or a pre-prepared module book containing the recommended reading materials. These have been compiled not just to give you something to do, but are created from relevant articles and chapters in books, each providing a different perspective on the subject, and will often include business examples to help you to apply the theory. The reading of these either before or after the lecture provides a deeper understanding and context for the subject. However, this does not mean that the lecture itself is redundant; lectures are very useful as they provide a learning environment for the following:

- to give you an overview of a topic area
- to help you understand the subject
- to help you make connections between different areas of study
- to show how to apply the concepts in a contemporary environment
- to engage you with key critical concepts
- to encourage you to read around the subject
- to enthuse and to motivate you.

Becoming an active learner

A good lecturer should encourage you to think about the subject and illustrate this with appropriate examples. As a member of the audience, it is very easy to sit listening while occasionally allowing your mind to wander. This is at best passive learning. To be effective, you should engage and be active in the learning process. This requires that you prepare yourself before a lecture, be attentive during the lecture, think about what is being said, write notes and reflect on them afterwards.

> **Note**
>
> Occasionally, you might look at the topic of a lecture and think to yourself, 'not this again!', 'I did this last year', or 'I did this in a different module!' In a broad subject like business strategy, there are many areas that are shared with other business modules. The lecture title may well be similar, but the direction of approach, examples and delivery are likely to be very different. Even if some of the content is familiar to you, it does no harm to listen to another lecturer discussing the subject. At worst, it will be a useful revision, and most likely it will add useful additional information and an alternative perspective to the subject.

Making the best use of your lecture's learning outcomes

Before the lecture, your lecturer will often provide the lecture contents, most commonly slides and possibly also the background notes. Print these out in a suitable format so that you have space to write on them during the lecture and can highlight key areas for further study. The learning process is also helped by the availability of the key academic concepts which are also called the learning outcomes. The learning outcomes are the focus of the lecture. The majority of what is delivered will be based on these, but this does not mean that this is all you will learn! Knowing the learning outcomes and the content of the lectures provides you with the opportunity to do some preparative reading. There are many advantages to this:

- It will give you a useful perspective on what is going to be taught.
- It will position the subject in a wider context of your studies.
- It will give you advance notice if something is likely to need particular attention.
- It will mean less note-taking in the lecture.
- You will be concentrating on the detail of the lecture rather than getting to grips with the basic concepts.
- You will not be tempted to copy down the slides.
- It will save you time reading after the lecture.

You may also wish to write questions for yourself prior to the lecture so that you can answer these as the lecture is delivered. If there are any aspects of the lecture that you are unsure of, for example, the use of terminology, make a note on your printout and then be sure to ask your tutor or look it up in your textbook, possibly in the glossary before the lecture. As soon as you can after the lecture, write up these notes, add information from other sources and highlight the key concepts.

This whole process may seem somewhat long-winded but it will reap great dividends both during your studies and at examination time. It also provides the opportunity for reflection which helps to reinforce the memory. You gain a deeper understanding, learning becomes more meaningful and revision becomes so much easier. Many of the concepts that you learn in your lecture will also be practised in seminars and tutorials.

> You may find that in the first few weeks of studying the subject, there are so many new terms that it is difficult to understand what is being said. Don't worry too much. Ask or look them up and memorise them before or after the lecture and you will soon find that you are using them yourself!

Asking questions in lectures can be very daunting, especially in a large class, but your lecturers will often welcome questions as it gives them an opportunity to break from the lecture and focus on something that you (and most probably other students) are finding difficult. It also shows that you are listening and will often influence their focus when delivering subsequent lectures or tutorials. Attract your lecturer's attention, by putting your hand up and when prompted, speak loudly and clearly so everyone can hear and you don't have to repeat yourself. You might find it helpful to write your question down when you think of it just in case you forget later.

Taking effective notes in lectures

Taking notes in lectures is essential, but how you do this is very much down to the individual's preference and may solely be influenced by your writing speed and ability to read your own shorthand! However you take notes, there should be an appropriate balance between listening to what is being said, understanding it and summarising it in your own way. Do not try to write everything that is being said; you will not be able to write fast enough and certainly not be able to follow the lecture in enough detail to learn from it.

> **Note**
>
> Some students record lectures. This must be approved by the lecturer, so ask before the lecture starts as permission may be refused. Your university's policy will probably also state that it must be only for your own use, as ultimately the lecture is the copyright of the lecturer or university. If you do record the lecture, you will still need to make notes from the recording but at least you can pause and rewind!

Below are 12 tips which you may find useful when taking lecture notes:

1 Practise different forms of note-taking and use the one that works best for you.

2 Ensure that you are mainly listening, thinking and summarising rather than just writing.

3 Use your own words after you have thought about what has been said.

4 Develop your own form of shorthand, such as symbols, arrows and abbreviations. You might find it useful to occasionally use SMS (text) jargon!

5 Diagrams such as mind-maps often help in complex areas where many connections need to be made.

6 Write phrases and key words rather than sentences.

7 Use bullet points or numbered lists whenever you can. Look for clues from the lecturer, such as *'There are a number of view-points on this...'*.

8 Don't waste time writing down what is on the slides if they are made available to you before or after the lecture.

9 Always re-write your notes in tidy writing (or word process them) as soon as you can after the lecture and while it is still fresh in your mind. This is the ideal time to memorise the content with minimal effort. A week later it may mean very little.

10 Swap notes with your friends. Often you will have each spotted something that the other has missed.

11 Take the opportunity to add to these notes as you read around the subject.

12 Put page numbers on your notes in case they become separated.

Links to transferable skills

In a work environment, the skills of preparation, writing while listening, summarising key points, information management and note-taking will be particularly important when attending presentations, writing reports and summarising or preparing meeting minutes. As with most skills, they will develop over time as you find new ways to optimise them for your own purposes.

3.7	
making the most of your seminars	

This section will show you how to:

- benefit from seminar activities
- contribute to debate in seminars
- work in groups
- deal with group problems.

Benefiting from seminar activities

While seminars vary greatly in content and style, there are some common themes. For example, the group sizes are often small, usually between 10 and 30 students and the emphasis is on discussion and debate of previously taught material, either through presentations or group work. Seminars may be timetabled less frequently than lectures, but this should not devalue their importance as they are a chance to:

- reinforce or apply what has been taught in lectures
- ask questions and to test your understanding
- evaluate different perspectives
- practise examination questions
- practise teamwork, debating and presentation skills
- identify problems that you may not have considered
- practise your presentation skills.

Seminars are certainly not suitable for the passive learner since sitting and listening will not help you to develop or practise these skills. Business strategy seminars will commonly require the pre-reading of a business case or for you to research a business or industry. Preparation is therefore particularly important and you should come equipped with the appropriate material and notes in order to optimise your experience. You will note many similarities between the content and structure of seminars and strategy examinations. You may even find that your seminar discussions are using previous examination cases and questions. Make use of this opportunity to get some practice!

If you are unused to participating in class, a seminar is a good place to start. You might start by asking or answering a question or by disagreeing with what has already been said. In the end it doesn't matter, as you will see that it is not difficult to contribute, and with each occasion your contribution will become even easier. Make an effort to be one of the first to speak in the following seminar in order to keep up the momentum. The more practice you get in this small environment, the more comfortable you will be in other more demanding circumstances.

Contributing to debate in seminars

When debating in seminars, make sure that you remember to give the other side a chance to make their case. Invariably, there are at least two sides to every argument and they may be equally valid but in different ways. Do not get aggressive or personal, and if you find yourself raising your voice, stop talking. The purpose of the seminar is to get as many perspectives as possible, not to win an argument! Also allow other students to make their point. Even if they are not so articulate, they will often have something valuable to contribute. Most importantly, listen closely to what the others have to say, consider how you are going to respond and avoid the temptation to interrupt the speaker.

Working in groups

Group work often provides new challenges to students, particularly those who work well on their own and are uncomfortable when relying on the input from others. However, group or team work is commonplace and many of the challenges that occur in a university context will also be present in a work environment. In fact, interpersonal skills are so important to prospective employers that they ask at interview if you have experience working in teams and how you coped! Working co-operatively also provides many of the following useful benefits:

- It brings together a wide range of experience and perspectives.
- It is an opportunity to test ideas.
- It can be creative.
- It exposes you to other thought processes, perspectives and possibly different cultures.
- While the rest of the group is talking, it provides you with the opportunity to think.
- It allows you to practise all of your skills.

- It provides the opportunity to make new friends.
- It is a useful soft skill to develop, which is highly valued by employers.

Often your group may be selected for you. If this is the case, it is usually with the intention to separate friends and mix nationalities. This promotes individual development by taking you out of your comfort zone and mixing you with very different people and cultures. To be a productive group member, you will need to develop your interpersonal skills. This includes being supportive, listening well, making suggestions, offering constructive criticism, receiving criticism and being equitable when sharing out tasks, etc. Daniel Goleman (1995) characterised these traits as having Emotional Intelligence or the ability to understand and manage your own and other people's emotions, feelings and motivations. Some people are naturally very good at this, but most of us have to work at it, particularly when working in groups.

Note

When meeting in a group for the first time, it is possible that you are all new to each other. This will naturally slow proceedings down at first but very quickly you will each develop an opinion of each other. It is important not to stereotype or ignore people when you first meet them, as often those whom you think are quiet or perhaps uninteresting turn out to be the most important contributors.

Your group may be tasked to complete a report, poster, project or presentation, so at the first meeting discussions need to take place on how best to proceed, what needs to be completed and who should do what. It is best to break a large project down into its individual tasks, but be aware that some tasks may not be immediately apparent and others may have to be completed in sequence. To illustrate this, we can use an example – for instance, if you are required to make a presentation on the culture of an organisation, the following tasks will need to be completed:

1 The overall content will need to be determined and is likely to consist of both academic theory and the background to the organisation.

2 You need to develop a 'skeleton structure' of the contents (even if you change it later).

3 You need to decide who does what research.

4   The main topic areas then need to be researched and subdivided.

5   You need to decide how best to apply the theory to the organisational example.

6   You need to decide on how much detail you need to provide in each section in order to cover all the topic areas but keep within the allocated time.

7   An introduction and conclusion need to be written.

8   The content has to be clearly mapped on to slides and notes.

9   The presentation needs to be designed and formatted.

10   A decision has to be made on who presents what and who introduces the group.

11   A practice session needs to be organised and timed, leaving sufficient time for corrections to be made.

12   The presentation is delivered.

These tasks are in addition to the usual group maintenance of how often, when and where you meet, how you get in touch with each other and who has access to resources (e.g. computer, internet, memory stick, library, etc.). In the early stages of project planning, brainstorming is a very useful tool, particularly to get everyone working together and to generate ideas or content that can be categorised and structured later.

> **Note**
>
> Don't forget the basic rules of brainstorming: all input is acceptable, criticism is not allowed and discussion takes place only after the session.

When allocating tasks, consider what your and the other group members' strengths are. If, for example, a member of the group is particularly good at graphic design, it makes sense for this person to develop the presentation materials but as a result their contribution to the research may be less. You may find Meredith Belbin's work on team role classification useful when identifying key traits in your group members (Belbin, 1993). The purpose of the classification is to recognise the characteristics of both yourself and the other group members and identify the useful functions each can play in the group.

- **Implementer.** This is a doer; they work hard but often require detailed instructions which they will then thoroughly perform. They can be indecisive.
- **Coordinator.** This is one of the leaders in a group; they are neutral, fair and take contributions from all members, but are happy not to take control. They can be dispassionate.
- **Shaper.** This is a leader who is driven by a desire to get the job done and often influences the decision-making of the group. They can be intolerant.
- **Innovator.** This will be a creative member of the group, capable of lateral thinking and sometimes wacky in their approach or ideas. They may be quiet, unconventional and highly intelligent. They are not a detail person and can be unrealistic.
- **Resource investigator.** A confident group member who is happy to search or ask for help or resources. They may be over-optimistic in their plans.
- **Monitor-evaluator.** This is the equivalent of the book-keeper of the team, someone who likes to monitor progress and track developments (often financial). They can be very critical and negative.
- **Team worker.** This person is most likely to be concerned with how the team interacts and works together; they will strive to ensure harmony and cohesion, but they can easily be influenced by other group members.
- **Completer-finisher.** This person will worry about completing tasks on time and will check the progress of others to ensure that they are not held back. They will often want to complete the project well before the deadline in order to allow for unforeseen delays. They are often unable to delegate and are too engrossed in the detail.
- **Specialist.** These are people brought in to help on a particular task (e.g. an IT specialist). They are often very focused on their specialism and often cannot see the wider implications of the project.

You might appreciate that in a well-balanced group, each of these characteristics would be useful, but it is unlikely that they will all be present. Indeed, some projects require more of a particular characteristic than others, but few groups would survive if all the members were monitor-evaluators!

> **Note**
>
> Over time, you will gain an appreciation of each of the group members. It is said that everyone has something to give and sometimes it is just a case of discovering what that might be!

Dealing with group problems

It is common that groups do not work effectively. For example, group members may not come to meetings, they may turn up late, they do not complete their task or perhaps they are argumentative. In both a university or work environment, this can lead to high emotions, particularly if your individual performance is likely to be affected by the group's overall performance. This realisation can manifest itself as anger or frustration and even tears.

There are a number of factors which can cause these emotional responses:

1 Differing opinions which may be either:

- personal or
- subject-related.

2 The working of the group, for example:

- unfair task allocation
- views not being considered or taken seriously
- absenteeism, non-communication or late arrival
- lack of contribution
- poor or late task completion.

3 Events from outside the group, such as changing timescales, scope of the project or lack of resources.

Outside events will include anything that the group doesn't have control over and will have to be managed by the group just as they would in any work environment. These challenges are all part of group work and should be approached in a mature and constructive manner – with group work, successful project completion is more important than relationships within the group.

Successful groups often have a strong and respected leader who ensures equal contribution and leads by example. If an individual is not pulling their weight, then it is the group's responsibility to sort the problem out in a professional manner. Group rules should also stipulate that differences of opinion are welcome but they should be handled independently from the person who holds the opinion.

Note

The ultimate sanction for unacceptable behaviour might be to expel the offender from the group, but you will have to check what your tutor thinks of this solution! Bear in mind that in a work environment, there is no alternative to the group professionally managing problems like this, so view it as useful practice.

You might find the following 12 tips useful to encourage effective group membership. You could also use these as the basis for group 'rules'.

1 Listen carefully to others.

2 Do not dismiss opinions without full consideration.

3 Be encouraging to others.

4 Be diplomatic and polite when disagreeing with another group member.

5 Include everyone in the decision-making.

6 Do not dominate the meeting.

7 Complete your own tasks on time.

8 Keep to the subject, and try to avoid digression.

9   Admit your mistakes.

10   If you don't understand what has been discussed or decided upon, ask for confirmation.

11   Summarise discussions and document the outcomes, perhaps copying in group members by email.

12   Ensure that everyone knows what they are going to do and when and where you are next going to meet.

Links to transferable skills

Group work is the 'bread and butter' of the workplace. As organisations are increasingly project- and team-orientated, so you are likely to be working with a variety of people from different nationalities and backgrounds. Working in groups provides experience of taking directions from others, taking personal responsibility, helping to solve problems and maintaining group harmony.

3.8	
essay writing techniques	

This section will show you how to:

- research and plan your essay
- format your essay
- deconstruct a title or question
- keep within your word count.

You will have been writing essays for some years, however it is surprising how poorly some students approach this task and it is often the structure rather than the content that is the problem. At this stage in your academic career, you will be expected to write several thousand words by bringing together information from a wide variety of business and academic sources. Putting this together in a logical and readable manner requires careful planning which is important because:

- it helps you to identify the important themes and the less important aspects
- it clarifies your thought processes
- it makes it more readable for your tutor and therefore easier to award higher marks
- it helps to avoid repetition and to control your word count
- it demonstrates a deep understanding and a logical mind, which is why this form of assessment is used!

Researching and planning your essay

Independent research is often a key ingredient to essay writing, but it is also a useful workplace skill, particularly when evaluating markets. The study of business strategy also provides an opportunity to research in one of two ways: primary research and secondary research.

Primary research is original research performed by the researcher in order to obtain answers to questions or to test a hypothesis.

Secondary research comes from existing sources of data, which might include books, articles, journals, databases, reports and previous research.

Primary data may be collected by some form of survey, interview or by observation. Secondary research provides information for writing essays. Secondary data is generally quicker to obtain than primary data but it will, by definition, be dated and collected for a different purpose.

When undertaking secondary research, use your library and the internet selectively or you will find yourself swamped by information, much of it only superficially relevant. Commonly, your research will start with books as the primary source of information and once you have gained a feel for the topic, you will move to more specific databases, journals and periodicals. In your library, find out the most appropriate journal databases for your search as this will improve both speed and focus. The careful use of keywords when using search engines will also greatly help in this respect, so it is worth spending time developing combinations and orders of words that best describe and filter your topic.

Most researchers prefer to print paper copies of articles: these provide both a permanent record and are also useful for highlighting and scribbling comments on. Don't forget to keep a careful record of all your sources of reference, perhaps by using a spreadsheet or custom software such as EndNote.

Formatting your essay

Essay planning and formatting is worth doing thoroughly: it will save you time in the long run and will gain you a better mark. Essays may be formatted in a number of ways and unless directed by your tutor this will be down to the preference of the student. However, all essays should be constructed like a sandwich, with the 'meat' in the middle. For example:

- **The introduction.** This provides the opportunity to 'set the scene' and review what you think the question is asking for and what you will write about. Don't waste too many words here as you will find that you will either be digressing from or repeating what you need to say later on. Many people find it is best to leave the introduction till last, when you know what you have written about!
- **The middle section.** This will be the longest and contain your arguments and discussions.
- **The conclusion.** This is your chance to bring everything together as a summary. It provides links back to the main arguments (theories and perspectives) and to the original title. It is vital that you get the length just right: too short and it will look hurried and you may have missed key points; too long and you may be repeating the middle content and wasting valuable word count!

Don't forget to regularly back up your work. Every few hours, back up your essay on a memory stick, CD or university server, or alternatively email it to yourself! This will ensure that you have a separate and retrievable copy. Many people find it easier to read and edit a printed copy rather than to do this on a screen, and of course it is also another form of back-up!

When writing essays, you will often be asked to compare or discuss different perspectives. The middle section may be formatted in one of two ways, the alternate or block mode, as shown in Figure 3.3.

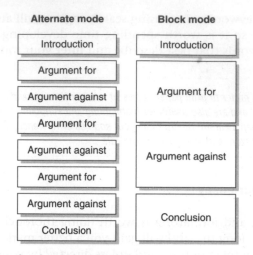

Figure 3.3   Ways to structure your essay

You might like to consider the alternate mode as being like a tennis match with yourself as referee. Each time the player hits the ball (or argues a point), the opponent will return with their argument. As a referee, you are there to ensure fair play and transparency and while you may have sympathy for a particular player (or argument), this should not get in the way of the game (or debate). Occasionally, an ace may be served, in which case there may not be a counter-argument in this respect. This is fine, as there is not always a counter-argument to everything and this should be stated.

> When comparing two perspectives, try to be objective and consider all the facts and evidence in an un-biased manner. You may feel strongly about the subject but that should not be evident from your writing. Critical thought and academic writing are discussed in more detail in separate chapters in this Course Companion.

If you feel that it is more appropriate or you are more comfortable in debating the full ranges of views in 'block mode', ensure that each argument is structured in a similar order so that cross-referencing can take place. The conclusion is particularly important in this mode as it is your opportunity to finally bring things together and to summarise your findings.

To prepare for an essay, you might find it useful to follow this 10-point guide to essay writing:

1 Ensure that you know what is required, what is relevant and what isn't. Deconstruct the title and highlight the important words (see later in this section).

2 Before you begin your research, create a quick list of the topics and content that you think will be relevant. You might find mind-mapping useful here (see section 3.5 on memory techniques).

3 From these, create a 'skeleton' contents list which you can add to or change as you progress.

4 Start searching relevant sources – from an academic perspective, it might be best to start with textbooks before moving to journals.

5 Ask yourself if the information you have found is directly relevant. If it is, add additional topics and headings to your 'skeleton' contents list as you proceed.

6 Optimise your contents list by grouping and linking similar subjects together under appropriate titles.

7 Write a draft essay using your contents list. Don't worry if at this stage you are over your word count. Write in a formal manner, avoiding slang and abbreviations.

8 Re-work your draft several times until only the essential elements are present and the word count is met. Deleting large blocks of 'hard-worked' text is always disheartening but often worth it!

9 Ensure that you have referenced correctly both in the text and in the reference list at the end (see section 3.9 on writing in an academic style).

10 Print out and quality-check the printed essay. You will be surprised how many mistakes you find when reading in a different format. Make sure that the final copy is formatted and positioned neatly on each page.

Deconstructing the title or question

Analysis of the title or question is perhaps one of the most important stages of the essay-writing process, so you need to deconstruct the title to fully understand what is required.

You can write the most wonderful prose for your essay but unless it is relevant you will not be awarded marks. Often there will be one or more key themes and often many sub-themes that require discussion, so make sure that these are covered and constantly refer back to them throughout your research to ensure that you are not drifting off the topic.

Depending on your essay title or question, you will find different keywords which provide an indication of the approach you should take. Some of the commonly used ones are listed below with a description of what is required:

- **Analyse.** Examine the key features in detail, possibly by using tools, frameworks and models, in order to provide useful information.
- **Contrast.** Identify the differences between two or more arguments and emphasise the relative importance of these. If appropriate, illustrate by providing examples.
- **Evaluate.** Analyse the relative importance or usefulness of something. Use evidence or examples to support your argument.
- **Illustrate.** Explain using examples.
- **Interpret.** What does it mean?
- **Justify.** Provide evidence to support the argument or case.
- **Relate.** Demonstrate connections, similarities or differences between two or more things.
- **Summarise.** Show the main points without the supporting detail or argument.
- **Synthesise.** Bringing together information from a variety of sources in order to create something unique.
- **Critically evaluate.** Analyse the strength of evidence from all sides of the argument. Which opinions or theories or models are most relevant and why?
- **Critically discuss.** Similar to critical evaluation. Which are the most important aspects and why? Consider the implications of what you are reasoning and provide arguments for and against.
- **To what extent.** Does the subject contribute something? You will need to discuss your findings and argue your case as to the extent of the proposition. Some aspects are likely to be supportive while others less so.

Identifying these words will help to set the tone of the essay. For example, a 'critical evaluation' might require you to evaluate (or analyse) using tools to provide data and conclusions. These are then compared and contrasted with the alternatives to provide the critical aspect of the evaluation.

When writing essays, there are 10 tips that lead to good practice:

1 Write in a formal manner; do not use slang or be too familiar.

2 Contrast the opinions or findings in an unbiased manner.

3 Do not state your own opinion unless asked. The viewpoints of authors are usually all that is required.

4 Make sure that you have a logical flow to your essay.

5 Be discursive by linking each sentence and paragraph to the previous sentence or paragraph. It makes it easier to read as it 'tells a story'.

6 Support your arguments with relevant and up-to-date evidence and data.

7 Use an academic writing style with detailed references (see section 3.9 on writing in an academic style for more information).

8 Show your awareness of how complex the situation is. In strategy, there is rarely a clear-cut demonstration of fact. Show the weaknesses in the different arguments, tools or analysis and in your own findings.

9 Don't be frightened to make assumptions, but clearly state when and why you have done so.

10 If asked to explain your conclusion, state why you came to this decision.

Keeping within the word count

Word-count limits on essays are normally used to ensure equality between students and to encourage concise writing, but this is also a skill that is very important in the workplace. It means that when you are writing an essay, you will have to be careful to ensure the relevance of the content and keep repetition to a minimum. This is particularly challenging in this age of instant access to seemingly unlimited information. However, essays are written texts so don't be tempted to resort to the use of lists and bullet points in order to save on word usage. Neither should you use an appendix as a repository for anything that should otherwise go in the main body of the essay! You might find the following 10 tips useful in reducing your word count:

1 If the content is not directly relevant to the question or title, delete it, or at least shorten it to be more concise and appropriate.

2 If you find yourself writing 'as I said before', you usually do not need to say it again or you need to restructure the essay so that you do not need to say it twice.

3 Look for alternative and shorter ways to say the same thing. Sometimes whole sentences can be removed without affecting the message.

4 Try to avoid a 'scatter-gun' approach of including everything in the hope that some of it will be relevant.

5 If you are not sure where a paragraph or sentence fits in your essay, consider leaving it out.

6 Look at your introduction to see if it can be shortened – often there are very few marks allocated to this section.

7 A good structure which groups related content together avoids repetition and reduces the word count.

8 Only use examples where they are directly relevant. Limit them to one or two good examples, which may demonstrate several points (i.e. look for quality rather than quantity).

9 Always condense detailed arguments into a small number of key themes.

10 Get someone else to read your final draft. If they don't understand sections, re-word or remove them.

> *Many institutions penalise the student for submitting word counts that are over the stated limit. However, if you have the opposite problem of not knowing where to start, read section 3.5 on the use of mind-maps.*

Links to transferable skills

Writing in a planned and structured manner is excellent practice for business, particularly if you are to write reports, reference manuals or standard operating procedures (SOPs). It is likely that you will also be required to present a written argument to a specific deadline and word count, and certainly the skills developed when logically structuring and quality-checking the detail will stand you in good stead. Keeping it short and to the point is an excellent skill to utilise in all forms of writing and will be greatly appreciated by your superiors!

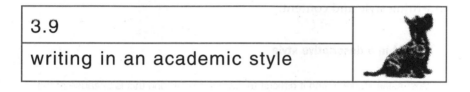

3.9
writing in an academic style

This section will show you how to:

- write critically
- avoid plagiarism
- reference within the text.

Writing from a critical perspective

There are a number of pitfalls when writing academic essays and the most common failure at final-year undergraduate level is a lack of criticality (see section 3.8 on writing essays and section 3.2 regarding critical thinking). This is why comments from course tutors such as 'too descriptive' or 'where is the debate?' often appear on feedback forms. A critical debate (either verbal or written) should contain the following elements:

- It argues a case based on the evidence.
- It puts forward differing points of view.
- It evaluates the significance of different points of view.
- It highlights the similarities and differences between different perspectives.
- It is un-biased in nature, and avoids personal opinion.

Note

In business strategy assignments, students often undertake the analysis and then produce a description of the main themes. They then neglect critical debate, which usually makes up the bulk of the marks.

In business strategy, you will be expected not only to read but also to write critically, presenting different perspectives from all sides of the argument. When considering each viewpoint, note down the key arguments that are being made and then review the opposing debate against them. Once you have completed your essay, don't forget to critically review it!

Below are two example paragraphs from the same assignment that is reviewing the educational differences between Asian higher education and western higher education. You should be able to see the difference in writing style and content.

Extract in a descriptive style

Most Asian students find it difficult to learn in the UK and this is because of the way they have been taught in the past. When western students learn, they initially learn by rote, which can be classed as a passive learning style, and then in higher education they are encouraged to learn for themselves by reading around the subject. This provides a deep understanding of the subject. Asian students, on the other hand, learn by rote or passive learning even in higher education – their tutors and textbooks provide all the knowledge they need to know. Western academics think that this form of higher education is old-fashioned and I do not think that it is a good way of learning.

While readable, this paragraph is highly subjective and considers only the author's narrow viewpoint, and because of this, it is lacking a range of supporting references. The flow of logic is also flawed. For example, if it is accepted that Asian students struggle with the UK educational system, then there are likely to be many other possible reasons which should be considered, other than rote learning, such as language or differing forms of assessment. It also makes assumptions about 'all' western academics which is an unsupported comment that is unlikely to be true: 'Western academics think that this form of higher education is old-fashioned.' Finally, the author's unsupported viewpoint is also inappropriate, biased and clearly unsupportable: '…I do not think that it is a good way of learning.'

Extract in a critical style

Asian students, when they are first taught in the UK, often find the education system challenging. Many of the misconceptions/preconceptions of Asian student learning behaviour are discussed by authors such as Biggs (1987) and Watkins & Hattie (1981), and include language, critical thinking and forms of assessment. One of the concerns is that learning by rote and passive learning are seen as appropriate only at the lower levels of the learning taxonomy (Biggs & Collis, 1982), rather than at higher levels of study, as is widely practised across Asia.

Hoefstede (1986) has described those students who are brought up in large power–distance societies (such as Asia) as tending to have teacher-centred classrooms, where the teacher is the respected expert who should not be criticised or challenged. This is perceived by some in the west as an 'old-fashioned' method of teaching which doesn't encourage deep learning, but evidence for this appears to be anecdotal. However, it has been demonstrated that under these conditions Asian students actually achieve higher levels of deep learning than they do in, for example, Australian institutions (Biggs, 1991). Controlled studies by Volet & Renshaw (1996) have also shown that Asian students are taught better in their home countries than they are in western countries. Furthermore, Hess & Azuma (1991) showed that Chinese students do tend to learn by rote and repetition but this can be used as an alternative route to deeper understanding. In conclusion, rote learning should not be automatically considered as an inappropriate means to developing deep learning. Contrary to some opinions, the evidence indicates that it can provide deep understanding of the subject, but further research needs to be undertaken to determine why this might be so.

The critically written extract supports each statement with links to research evidence. There is no obvious sign of bias or opinion, it admits that there are likely to be other influences on educational performance and has used a range of independent research on rote learning in Asia to support their conclusion. These sources can be checked in order to determine the relative validity of the research findings, for example, to determine the sample size of the survey. The concluding sentence neatly summarises the main argument and leaves the discussion open for further evaluation.

Avoiding plagiarism and poor academic practice

Plagiarism is the use of other people's words or ideas as your own (i.e. without identifying the original source).

Referencing is not just used to avoid plagiarism it is also required to demonstrate transparency, courtesy, thoroughness and to provide a useful aid to others when looking for the original source of information. You might also be charged with plagiarism if you only change the words from the original source, you must still reference the ideas to the original author. You can, of course, quote directly from another source. This may be done through quotation marks and the appropriate acknowledgement, but this should only apply to a sentence or two rather than paragraphs of text.

Another potential pitfall to academic writing is that some students find a passage of text from a secondary source and use it as a large part of their answer. Overall, the essay will have no structure as it is comprised of a 'patchwork quilt' of different quotes. If the answer contains large tracts of text from other sources, referenced or otherwise, it is clearly not the student's work, and serves only to demonstrate the student's ability to find and copy information. The tutor is looking for independent thought, the ability to understand the question and provide a relevant, well-constructed and coherent answer.

If your first language is not English, it may be tempting to use large blocks of text with a reference at the end, as you may feel that your own words may not be as eloquent as those in the copied text. But remember that your tutor will always prefer poor English grammar to someone else's formal text.

There are a number of things that you might practise in order to avoid the charge of plagiarism or academic misconduct.

1 Fully read a section of a document and summarise the main themes in your mind before you start to write notes.

2 Make an accurate reference of where you sourced the information. A spreadsheet is useful for this, as you can later cut and paste the reference into your essay.

3 Copy only those sentences that you will quote directly.

4 Use the referencing system exactly as your institution's guidelines state.

5 Ensure that your reference list is alphabetical by family name and not by initial or first names.

6 As a rough guide, you can expect that each paragraph has at least one and often several references in it.

Referencing within the text

There are a wide range of referencing standards and guidelines. Whichever convention you are required to use, you should try within your text to vary the phrasing when introducing authors in order to make the essay more readable. Below are some examples of phrases that you may wish to use:

- according to ...
- to quote from ...
- ... found that ...
- it has been claimed by ...
- ... states that ...
- however ... ascertains that ...
- ... makes the point that ...
- writing in 1999, ... argued that ...

> **Note**
>
> Plagiarism is a serious offence and if proven will usually result in the work not being marked and possible disqualification. If the student has used the occasional reference but only at the end of blocks of copied text, then it may not be considered as plagiarism, but it will certainly be classed as poor academic practice and will be marked down accordingly. Make sure you are familiar with your institution's guidelines and implement them exactly as required. These are easy marks to gain and lose.

Link to transferable skills

Critical writing is essential if your intention is to come across as unbiased and objective. When writing business reports, it is essential that you maintain your professional objectivity. Even if you are hoping for a particular outcome, the end result is that your report will be considered more seriously.

In most businesses, there is no requirement to reference in a detailed academic manner. However, all data and quotations should still be fully referenced so the reader can refer to the original source. If you intend to publish in academic journals or continue to study for a higher degree, or work in academia, accurate academic referencing is essential.

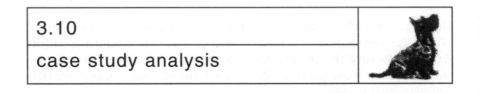

3.10	
case study analysis	

This section will show you how to:

- analyse a case study
- construct a case study answer.

Analysing a case study

Prior to writing your essay or sitting your exam, you will usually be required to research or analyse an industry or organisation and this will provide the information that you need to answer the question(s). This information is often given in the form of a pre-researched case study. Case studies commonly provide the following information, some of which may be in more depth than in others:

- a history of the strategic development of an organisation or industry
- information on the organisational structure, culture, financial situation and products
- current and potential strategic issues
- a discussion of one or more strategic implementations.

Note that these themes will be mixed with other less important information and possibly irrelevant information, so you will have to sort the 'wheat from the chaff' and decide what is relevant to your answer. There are many ways that you can analyse a case. Your own institution and textbooks may recommend different approaches, but you might find the following 10-step process a useful aid:

1 Quickly 'skim read' the case, without taking notes, in order to get an overview of the main themes. Ask yourself the following broad questions:

- What industry and markets are being discussed?

- Who are the major competitors?

- Are there key strategic decisions or strategic developments in its history that have caused changes in fortune?

- Does organisational culture play an important part, in a positive or negative way?

- What are the main issues that the organisation has to face, both internally and externally?

- Are the markets entering a growth phase or maturing?

- What is the possible future of the industry?

2 Re-read the case in more detail, highlighting with coloured pens the key passages that you think might be important and those that you will want to return to.

3 Draw a timeline of key events against the historical development of the company. Even if a question doesn't specifically ask for it, this is always useful as a short-cut to see trends which might not be so obvious from the text.

4 Go through the case again just looking for and noting information relating to one strategic theme at a time. These themes might relate to the chapter titles in this book and may include:

- external environment – opportunities and threats (e.g. PESTEL, Porter's five forces, Yip's globalisation drivers)

- internal environment – strengths and weaknesses (e.g. resource, core competence and financial analysis)

- value chain efficiencies or inefficiencies

- culture and change management

- organisational structure and important stakeholders (stakeholder mapping)

- competitive environment (e.g. generic strategies, strategic group analysis)
- product and market development (e.g. Ansoff matrix and BCG matrix)
- FDI or international market entry
- merger, acquisition and alliance activity, etc.

5   Analyse this information using appropriate tools and frameworks, selecting only the most relevant information to support your arguments. Look for links and interrelationships between theories and frameworks.

6   Analyse any tabulated data that you have, looking for trends from year to year (e.g. profitability of different product divisions). A detailed financial ratio analysis may be required, but even if it is not asked for, it may still provide additional evidence to support your arguments.

7   Check that you have not missed any nuances and make sure that you 'read between the lines' to find alternative meanings of what has been implied. For example, if an organisation is implementing a global computer network system, you can assume that communication, for example, of financial, marketing or supply chain data is a recognised problem. However, do not be tempted to place too much emphasis on material that is taken from the organisation's website, company spokespeople or publicity material, as this is likely to be somewhat biased.

8   Identify the strategic issues and strategic options that are open to the organisation, possibly in the form of a SWOT analysis.

9   Undertake a Suitability, Feasibility and Acceptability (SFA) analysis of each of these in order to conclude with a recommended strategic plan.

10   Finally, check that you can support all your arguments and conclusion with examples from your analysis and ensure that you have presented an unbiased perspective. Even your recommended strategic option will have risks attached, so make sure that these are highlighted and assessed.

This process does take some time, but is essential if you are to be able to provide a detailed analytically supportable answer to each question. Short-cutting the research and analysis always provides an incomplete picture and will reduce your marks accordingly.

Also think about what else you can contribute from your own knowledge. Often this can provide a starting point to other issues that you may want to consider. For example, if you are analysing the car industry, the case may not mention right-hand and left-hand drive cars, but this is clearly an important issue to a car manufacturer.

Constructing a case study answer

Once you have analysed the case and prepared your notes, you are ready to answer a question. There follows a mini-case study and an answer guide which should give you an indication of the nature of the content that is required when answering a strategy question. The following text is extracted from a number of internet sources. Material like this may either be provided to you or might be the product of your own research.

Mini case study notes

YKK's headquarters is in a small building in an unfashionable part of Tokyo. Nevertheless, this company is responsible for the manufacture of close to half the zippers in the world. Check your fly and it is likely that it says YKK on the tab! YKK has a global reach with 132 subsidiaries in 60 countries. Tadao Yoshida founded YKK in January 1946 but since 1990, YKK has been run by his son Tadahiro Yoshida. It is estimated that Yoshida and his family own 31% of the company, which equates to approximately $1.5 billion.

Their largest manufacturing facility in Japan is near Toyama, which boasts the ultra-efficient production of 7.2 billion zips/zippers a year. Common to all YKK's manufacturing plants is the self-reliance on its own value chain: integrated into their factories is the production of the teeth and grip of the zipper and the dye and yarn (cloth for the fabric of the zipper), and YKK even make the machines that make the zippers! The YKK factory site in Macon, USA, is the largest zipper factory in the world and produces 7 million zippers a day, in over 1500 styles and in more than 427 colours. Nevertheless, plastics and base metals are the only raw materials they need. The machines are highly automated with each component part being mechanically tested and potentially rejected by machines controlled by sophisticated software and without human intervention.

(Continued)

(Continued)

YKK opened its first shop in New York in 1960. At this time, the only orders they could attract were those that the competitors were not interested in, for example, unusual designs or colours. Over a period of time, they gained a reputation for a reliable, quick and flexible service. Other milestones include 1969, when YKK celebrated as the first man on the moon was wearing a space suit using YKK zippers. In the 1970s, Levi Strauss set a trend which moved from button flies to zippers on some jeans.

The main competitor, then as now, was Talon (Tag-It) in the USA, who invented the zipper. In those days, as the competitor's patents expired, YKK took the design, improved upon it and sold it at a competitive price. They were also ideally placed to supply the American garment manufactures as they moved into Asia. Today, the major competition comes from China, with over 1000 small companies competing in this market. Most of their competitors use manufacturing equipment which would be classed by YKK as old technology. However, it does provide a source of low-cost competition. In order to counter this, YKK has created a specific low-price brand to compete in these markets, with the emphasis on price rather than their usual standards of quality.

However, low-price competitors do not compete with YKK for business with multinational buyers like Levi Strauss, Adidas and Nike. Selling to companies such as these has meant that YKK has to ensure identical products and quality across the world (40 countries in the case of Adidas). This has come at a heavy cost in modernisation in all of YKK's Japanese and overseas plants.

YKK's product lines include:

- zippers
    - YZip: metal zipper, extra durable for jeans
    - Ever Bright: metal zipper, polished for visual appeal and corrosion resistance
    - Excella: metal zipper, polished and plated for visual appeal, also in different colours
    - Conceal: plastic coil zipper with no visible teeth
    - Vislon: rugged plastic zipper
- hook and loop products, more commonly known under the Velcro brand name of a competitor
- plastic parts, including various types of clip and buckle
- snaps and buttons, including snap fasteners and jeans buttons.

However, YKK are not reliant on fasteners for all their business. Other products, including architectural products such as aluminum products for windows and doors and the Machinery and Engineering Group, contribute significantly to the company. The Machinery and Engineering Group focuses on the development and production of machines, equipment and dies, serving the YKK Group with the Exclusive Machinery Division, Industrial Machinery Division and Die Division. The Group plays a key role in technology development which helps minimise costs while maximising efficiency to meet the changing, diversifying needs of the Fastening Products and Architectural Products Business Groups.

Extracts from the YKK Annual Report 2006

The organisation operates more than 123 affiliated companies in more than 70 countries, representing some 270 plants and offices with some 38,000 employees. Its geographical management structure is divided into six blocks:

1) North and Central America
2) South America
3) Europe, the Middle East, and Africa (EMEA)
4) East Asia
5) ASEAN countries, South Asia, and Oceania (ASAO)
6) Japan.

This regional approach enables YKK to adapt to the characteristics of each region and to further expand the businesses.

YKK Fastening Products Group

YKK's fastening products operations are divided into the Slide Fastener, Snap Fastener and Button, and Textile and Plastic Products Divisions. This structure enables us to respond flexibly to emerging market needs. YKK has always taken local characteristics into account and allowed marketing to be conducted more efficiently. Manufactured to rigorous quality-control standards within a vertically integrated production system, YKK controls every step of the manufacturing process to ensure quick response, prompt delivery and the highest possible quality at the lowest possible cost.

At YKK, we fully understand that our zippers are not end-use items; rather, they are critical components within our customers' products. The 'Textile & Plastic Parts

(Continued)

(Continued)

Division' covers three kinds of products. These are Hook & Loop, Webbing, and Plastic Parts. Including compounded products of these three, we also provide a wide variety of items aimed at creating a new market. At the six regions, we actively develop products based on the market needs of each region, and always challenge to create a new added value along with new demand.

In recent years, the world textile and apparel industries have seen considerable diversification in consumer needs, shorter product life cycles and demands for faster, lower-cost production. More nimbly to address these changes, we divided our global business into six geographical blocks, thereby enabling YKK to further contribute to our clients' globalisation efforts. Furthermore, *YKK Fastening Products Sales Inc.* considers Japan and the rest of Asia a single market and works towards more accurate product development and faster customer service.

The group faced a very severe situation such as skyrocketing raw material costs, mainly in metals, and shifting sewing production on a global basis during the fiscal year 2005. In the face of this business climate, we concluded that it is indispensable to speed up to meet changes and supported the product development by always maintaining one-step-ahead technological superiority.

We continued our project, targeting the domestic low-price products in ASEAN and South Asian markets, expanding to other regions as well, especially China. In the future, we will look at expansion to North, Central, and South America. R&D expenses related to this business totalled ¥6,858 million (US$59 million).

The **Architectural Products** Business Group manufactures *YKK AP* brand products, and does business in Japan and Asia as well as in the United States. Our production system features products developed to meet market needs precisely, manufactures to consistent standards and delivers a level of quality trusted around the world. The *YKK AP* brand aims to increase the value of buildings with entrance and window systems that offer quality, diversity, and uniqueness, based on the wide-ranging know-how we have accumulated through major projects around the world.

The **Machinery and Engineering** Group focuses on the development and production of machines, equipment and dies, serving *YKK Group* with the Exclusive Machinery Division, Industrial Machinery Division, and Die Division. The Group plays a key role in technology development and helps us minimise costs while maximising efficiency to meet the changing, diversifying needs of the Fastening Products and Architectural Products Business Groups.

The **Research & Development** Center works on metals, plastics and other new materials research as well as developing technology for applications processes. R&D activities benefit the entire *YKK Group*. Current projects include development of effective eco-friendly recycling technologies and other next-generation core technologies through which we can help create completely new value.

Counterfeit measures by YKK

Since the late 1970s, YKK have worked with counterfeit measures focusing on Hong Kong, Taiwan and China. However, along with the growth of the Chinese sewing industry in the 1990s, the focus on China has also been intensified. Within the global market they must also collaborate with the customers who import the garments. So in 1991, YKK established a Counterfeit Committee and began to actively promote counterfeit measures.

Five-year financial overview

Year ended 31st March	2002	2003	2004	2005	2006
Net sales (millions of yen)	364,554	473,307	557,852	581,973	619,612
Ordinary income (millions of yen)	16,475	20,639	30,846	32,554	33,826
Net income (millions of yen)	7,393	13,452	28,984	18,526	18,030
Shareholders' equity (millions of yen)	361,306	379,724	402,062	420,277	467,391
Total assets (millions of yen)	680,852	755,137	758,643	779,803	810,070
Shareholders' equity per share (yen)	317,284	323,143	337,169	352,418	389,684
Net income per share (yen)	6,704	11,611	24,571	15,435	14,959
Equity ratio (%)	53.1	50.3	53.0	53.9	57.7
Cash flows from operating activities (millions of yen)	40,767	55,629	67,619	64,056	51,678
Cash flows from investing activities (millions of yen)	Δ42,685	Δ22,988	Δ39,212	Δ32,697	Δ50,376
Cash flows from financing activities (millions of yen)	2,103	Δ22,406	Δ20,709	Δ13,395	Δ14,374
Cash and cash equivalents at end of year (millions of yen)	49,444	65,164	71,405	89,208	80,223
Number of employees (persons)	28,387	35,149	35,551	37,081	38,398

1 GBP = Approx 240 Yen

Example essay question:

Using appropriate frameworks, critically evaluate the global influences and the changing nature of the industry on YKK's strategic development.

The first item on the essay writing checklist is to deconstruct the question. As previously described, you should look for keywords in order to influence your content. The following four phrases are imperative to this question:

- *appropriate frameworks*
- *critically evaluate*
- *industry changes*
- *global influences on YKK.*

From these phrases, you can determine that you are expected to use strategic frameworks in an unbiased and thorough manner while questioning the validity of the information. These frameworks will enable you to determine what the global influences are. You are then to decide how they are likely to change the industry and in particular to identify the impact on YKK. Be aware that much of the information provided in the mini-case was from company sources and should be considered as one-sided.

PESTEL, Porter's five forces and Yip's globalisation driver frameworks are the most appropriate frameworks to use in the main body of your answer. However, an introduction showing that you understand the industries that YKK are involved in and the world markets that they serve will be expected. Strategic group analysis will be a useful tool here, as it can be used to demonstrate an understanding of the product groups and how these relate to different markets. Bring out the fact that the customers are also other businesses (B2B) that use a variety of fasteners as a component part in their own products. Low-cost, adaptability, reliability of supply and quality of the product are therefore very important in these markets. These can be illustrated by the introduction of a lower-cost (basic quality) YKK zipper product.

Apart from the fastener industry, you should also mention the construction and machinery businesses as these are a major source of revenue and growth for YKK. However, there is less supporting material in the case study for a detailed discussion beyond the link to the growth in building construction especially in China and India, and the potential benefits to the company with knowledge and technology leverage. The ability to reduce risk in rapidly changing global markets by cross-subsidising between the construction and fasteners business should provide financial stability and a sustainable competitive advantage to YKK.

The following are some of the major points from the analytical frameworks that should be embedded in main body of your answer.

Clues on the PESTEL factors can be identified in Yoshida's message and YKK's history, for example YKK's concerns over rising fuel and raw material (e.g. metal) costs, the ending of patent life, counterfeiting, etc. While these concerns are company-specific, they will impact on many industries and in your answer they should be critically evaluated, as to their relative impact. The importance of technology to the industry should also be highlighted with particular emphasis on the importance of automation/software for the reduction of manufacturing costs and improvement of quality. You can support this by the high level of R&D investment, but also by identifying that sales have increased but profitability has remained flat (five-year financial overview). You should also identify that the Chinese market is large and growing but low-cost counterfeiting is also a major issue. Expand on this theme, explaining why this should be.

Porter's five forces should show that the industry and YKK place a heavy reliance on the fully integrated value chain and therefore depends on only a few outside suppliers, which gives them demonstrable control over quality and costs. Large buyers, for example, global clothing brands based in Asia, will clearly purchase in larger volumes than smaller ones, and therefore wield more power over their suppliers. Competition is on a global scale and in a mature market, but the market also has many niches which gives room for small-scale, locally based competition. Hence, awareness, flexibility and speed when targeting new niches are vital in order to sustain the competitive strategy of the major players. The threat of new entrants is high due to the availability of manufacturing equipment and other technologies with relatively low capital expenditure. However, this currently has a minimal impact on the industry due to the global presence and reputation of large companies such as YKK. There are also numerous fastener substitutes, but many of these alternatives are widely sold throughout the industry (including YKK). Global players therefore need to keep abreast of design and technology to ensure that they don't miss new trends.

Yip's drivers will detail the global nature of the market which is predominantly based on similar needs and therefore provides the opportunities for economies of scale and scope. The retail price of the final product is low so automation and the leverage of technologies and materials from related industries are important – this is a competitive advantage of YKK. Branding plays an important part in global industries and it is important that YKK maintains its reputation for quality and leading-edge technology as part of their core competences. YKK is being driven into a globalised company due to the requirements of its global customers, demanding similar world-wide standards and lower prices which are linked to higher volumes. Political/government factors can be linked to PESTEL, with trade barriers, safety standards and textile agreements and so on being discussed.

The competitive nature of the market should be based on the findings of the analysis of the global market segmentation, with the major competitors broadly matching YKK's portfolio and global presence and mostly selling to global clothing brands. Porter's five forces can be linked to Yip's drivers as global competitive advantage is maintained predominantly by cost leadership supported by vertical integration and large-scale production. There are also important links to the value chain and value networks which provide the opportunity for extra marks.

Note

These brief pointers for your answer should be enhanced with examples and in particular with a justification of why they are so important to the company. Attempt to link each of your analysis outcomes with your findings and with other frameworks as this provides a more coherent answer.

Finally, conclude by returning to the question with a summary of the key influences on the industry, possibly using the external parts of a SWOT analysis. Opportunities should include the continued growth of 'global brand' clothing manufacturing in Asia, new fastener design opportunities, enhancement of economies of scale and global brand presence as a competitive tool. Threats will include the rapidly changing market, with new products reducing the opportunity to optimise for economies of scale. In addition, the increasing raw material costs and the distraction of the resource-intensive counterfeiting battles are likely to remain as threats into the future.

Links to transferable skills

While many of these strategic frameworks are used in industry, it is quite probable that few readers will in the future need to undertake a strategic analysis. However, there is every likelihood that the skills that you have developed in compiling, prioritising and critically analysing data will be vital when using business and market reports.

3.11	
presentation and examination hints and tips	

This section will show you how to:

- prepare and deliver a presentation
- revise for an examination
- prepare for an examination
- improve your examination technique.

Preparing and delivering presentations

If you are required to do an informal or assessed presentation, preparation is obviously very important. It is common to be stressed at the prospect, but your stress level will be reduced if you are comfortable with the subject and you focus on telling 'a story' rather than concentrating on the slides. The following list comprises 20 useful tips for preparing and giving your presentation:

1 Make sure that your presentation has a beginning, a middle and an end (i.e. it tells the listener what they are going to hear, it tells them about it and then it summarises it).

2 Break the presentation into sub-headings in order to give your presentation a logical structure.

3 Don't forget that you don't always have to use slides!

4 If you are using slides, don't be tempted to completely fill them with text.

5 Make sure the content is appropriate and at the right level for the audience. Rarely can you use the same presentation for different types of audience.

6 Make the slides clear and relatively free from animation and moving graphics as these have a habit of not working or distracting from the core message.

7 Illustrate your presentation with examples, as these help to break the flow and provide added interest.

8 If required, write the briefest notes or prompts on cards to act as reminders of key topics. Note that large pieces of paper exaggerate shaking hands!

9 Practise the presentation by timing yourself to ensure that you are within your guide-time.

10 Arrive in plenty of time to run through the slides and test the technical facilities.

11 Face the audience not the screen.

12 Take a deep breath and smile.

13 Breathe normally and speak slowly and clearly. Don't be afraid to pause and think.

14 Pretend to be confident – it usually helps!

15 Create your own words, tell it as a story. Do not be tempted to read the slides or your notes and certainly do not memorise it all – your mind is liable to go blank!

16 Attempt to make eye contact around the audience.

17 Remember that moderate movement often helps you to think and provides more interest to the audience.

18 Concentrate on what you are saying rather than on any other distractions.

19 Try to avoid humour in case it backfires or offends someone.

20 Try to be passionate about what you are saying.

It should be easy, but actually for most people it isn't, and to make it look easy always takes practice. Even the best presenters were nervous when they started out and still have bad days. So don't expect presenting to always be a good experience but remember that any mistakes that you make are often less noticeable to the audience than they are to you. In time and with practice, you may find that you actually enjoy the experience!

> **Note**
>
> Presenting is such an important transferable skill that you should volunteer to present as often as possible as you can't have too much practice. One day your presentation may be very important – apart from being assessed, it may lead you to a job or promotion – so it is much better to get your practice in a setting like a classroom rather than in front of an interview panel!

Revising for an examination

Examinations are designed to test your knowledge, understanding and ability. This is under controlled conditions to ensure that what you produce is entirely your own. However, at the final stages of undergraduate education, the testing of a deep understanding and the ability to extrapolate information, critically debate and problem solve, is more important than testing for the retrieval of facts. It is for this reason that many examinations allow additional aids, including:

- textbooks
- lecture notes
- case study materials
- restricted written notes on the case study.

Your examination guidelines should be closely followed to avoid disqualification. In the case of business strategy examinations, you are often provided with the topic to research or a pre-prepared case study prior to the examination so that you can analyse it and write notes. You would then be expected to use these notes in the examination as a basis for the questions that you will be asked.

Note

Many students prefer assignments (take-home essays) to exams as they feel more in control and are therefore less stressed than under examination conditions. However, it is worth remembering that exam submissions are often marked more leniently than assignments due to the imposed time limitation. Also, you are not required to reference in detail and poor structure, writing, grammar and spelling mistakes incur less penalties. In addition, an exam is over in a few hours without days or weeks spent agonising over the content, wording and word count.

You will generally know well in advance when your examination is likely to be. Use this time to organise and supplement your notes from other sources, although it will be much easier if you have been doing this after each teaching session. Make sure that you look at all the past examination papers – you are bound to find trends and recurring questions over time. In business strategy, the questions are most likely to be on set topics (see the examples in this Course Companion), so practice in seminars and tutorials is vital in order to determine what your tutor expects. Often, seminars are based around questions from past papers so this provides a good opportunity to get familiar with the expectations of your tutor.

If you are not allowed to take in any form of notes, write down all the frameworks and headings that you need to know (your Course Companion will be particularly useful here), attempt to memorise them and write them out from memory until you get them all correct. Section 3.5 on memory techniques will help you in this process. However, it is hoped that by the time you get to your exams, you will be so familiar with the theory, having used it so often, that you will have little cramming to do at the end.

Some revision do's and don'ts are listed below:

Do's

- **Plan well in advance.** See section 3.3 on time management.
- **Motivate yourself.** Do this by setting achievable targets and giving yourself small rewards. See section 3.3 on motivation.

- **Write notes as you revise.** Passing the information through your brain, synthesising it, and transferring it back to paper to be viewed again is very helpful, particularly if it is in the form of numbered lists, bulleted points or pictures.
- **Revise at every opportunity.** It is surprising how much you can learn every day in a 15-minute bus journey! Always carry some notes with you.
- **Use interactive learning techniques.** See section 3.5 on memory techniques.
- **Practise past papers.** You don't have to fully answer them, just get the main points down.
- **Revise with friends.** You can quiz each other, compare notes on how to answer particular questions and generally check your understanding.
- **Test your memory.** Be pleased if you find that you have forgotten something – it is better to re-learn it before the exam than realise that you have forgotten it in the exam!
- **Take care of yourself.** Gentle exercise in fresh air and a balanced diet improve concentration. Every half hour, stretch and walk somewhere, such as going to the corner shop, or to the kitchen to make a drink.
- **Practise writing at speed.** This is a skill developed over time but can still be practised when writing revision notes.
- **Attend all your end-of-year lectures and seminars.** If there are going to be any hints and tips or revision sessions, this is when your tutor will have planned them.

Don'ts

- **Leave it to the last minute.** Many students convince themselves that there is not much to learn and only realise that there is more than they thought when they actually sit down to revise! Start early and if you finish early that leaves time for other things. Writing notes and reading around the subject as the course progresses will not only gain you better marks, but it will also be less time-consuming and stressful at the end. Business strategy is best absorbed and practised over a long period.
- **Try to do too much at once.** Short intense periods are better than full days.
- **Re-read your notes over and over again.** The learning process requires stimulation from a number of senses; the brain is not actively learning if it is merely reading. See section 3.5 on memory techniques and section 3.6 on making the most of your lecture notes.
- **Make excuses for not revising.** At revision time, even tidying your room is more interesting!
- **Write model essays and learn them by heart.** This takes time and doesn't contribute to deep learning. If an unexpected question comes up, what do you do?
- **Assume because you have already revised it, that you will know it for the exam**. Re-test yourself on material that you have previously learned. It is natural to forget some things but fortunately it is easier to re-learn a second time.

Preparing for an examination

Don't leave your examination preparation, such as finding out when the examination is, to the last minute. Nor should you rely on friends for this information as they are not always as reliable as you are! Check where your examination room is and if you are not familiar with it, visit it in advance to make sure it is where you expected it to be. Check what you need to take into the exam (e.g. calculators, notes, ID card, etc.). If you are an international student, check on your institution's procedures and regulations when using language dictionaries and electronic translators. Put everything together the night before and try to get a good night's sleep.

Have a good breakfast, preferably consisting of slow-release complex carbohydrates such as cereals, bread and fruit. Slow-release foods provide a constant source of glucose to the brain which reduces mood swings and fatigue. Finally, anticipate delays and leave plenty of time for travelling. It is better to arrive very early and have time to mentally prepare yourself than to get there late and stressed.

There is good evidence to show that Ginseng improves long-term concentration by improving the blood flow to the brain, but I would suggest that if you use this for the first time, try it well before the day of the examination in case it doesn't agree with you!

Improving your examination technique

If you prepare for your strategy exam and have an expectation of the questions, there should be few surprises. However, mistakes can still be made in the heat of the moment so examination technique is important. The following list should help you to avoid the pitfalls when in the examination:

- Fill in your student details clearly.
- Read the instructions carefully, and make sure you know if the questions are compulsory or optional.
- Read the whole paper, particularly paying attention to the mark allocation.
- Calculate how long you should spend on each question, right down to what time you should be starting each question. Regardless of how comfortable you feel with answering it, do not be tempted to spend excessive time on a question with only a few allocated marks.
- Decide the order in which you will answer the questions, but don't forget that often strategy case study questions are constructed in a logical order so analysis and findings build sequentially from one question to another.

- If in doubt, start with the question you think is easiest as this will get you started and should get your get creative juices flowing!
- Deconstruct the questions and jot down the main themes for each. There should be a different focus for each of your answers.
- On spare paper, briefly mind-map your answers. This will save you time and improve your structure, and you can add to it as you think of things.
- Make sure that you clearly identify the question number and where each answer finishes.
- Use the essay writing techniques to format your answer. Try to make your reasoning clear and well structured and identify the key authors wherever possible.
- Avoid writing long 'flowery' introductions. These will rarely be awarded marks.
- Don't worry if it looks as though others are writing more than you, or seem to have finished early. There can be all sorts of reasons for this and not all of them are good!
- Don't be tempted to write everything you know on the topic as you will probably run out of time. Be selective and regularly remind yourself what the question is asking for. Anything else will not be marked. Remember: quality not quantity!
- If you find you are running out of time, resort to bullet points. You may salvage a few extra marks even if the structure is inappropriate. If you run out of time, say so at the end.

When completing a multiple-choice or short-answer examination, many of the above tips will also be relevant. However, with these examinations, you are more likely to answer the questions in an order with which you feel most confident, leaving the 'difficult ones' to last. Allocation of time to each question is just as important as the careful deconstruction of the question or statement. For example, watch out for statements with the words 'not' or 'least/most' in the question, as these will have a big impact on your answer! Make sure that you follow the conventions for multiple-choice answer sheets (i.e. if you are required to fill in a circle with a pencil, make sure you do this – an optical reader may not recognise a blue cross). Make sure you have lined up your answers with the correct question numbers and unless negative marking is used, attempt all the questions.

Links to transferable skills

It is highly likely that you will be required to do presentations in your workplace, even if the audience is only your direct work group and you are required to bring them up to date with the latest figures, activities or problems. However, presentation skills are also a vital tool in persuading and influencing others, or in making a case, particularly in a sales situation.

You may find it more difficult to see an equivalent experience in the workplace for examination technique. However, learning is clearly something that will always be important throughout your life, as is planning, working to deadlines and managing stressful situations. Admittedly, examinations are a somewhat artificial way to developing these experiences, but you will certainly come across situations during your career where you will feel that you are under the same pressure!

glossary

Acceptability of strategy	an evaluation of the stakeholder's likely approval of the strategic proposal.
Acquisition	or takeover, is the outright purchase of one organisation by another.
Asset specificity	the inability to use a resource for a task other than it was designed for. Asset specificity within a negotiated transaction can lead to an artificially high price as a result of opportunistic behavior on the part of the seller.
Audit	a process to check the validity and reliability of information. Typically, audits are applied to financial, environmental and other resources.
Barrier to entry	represents the difficulty in entering a market or sector.
Benchmarking	a comparison of performance with those best in class, with a view to identifying competitive advantages.
Bounded rationality	limitations on decision making due to previous experience, limited knowledge and high complexity.
Break-even analysis	a form of sensitivity analysis that is used to determine when the total expenditure equals generated profit.

Bureaucracy	the structure and processes created to ensure standardisation and control in an organisation.
Business-level strategy	the level of strategy predominantly concerned with the building of competitive advantage through product development in specific markets.
Business strategy	the management of the organisation's resources and competences in order to match the aims of the organisation and the threats and opportunities in the environment.
Change agents	typically, employees or consultants who are charged with supporting the implementation of the strategy and identifying potential implementation problems.
Competition Commission	an independent UK public body that investigates mergers, acquisitions and regulates major industries. Formerly known as the Monopolies and Mergers Commission.
Competitive advantage	an advantage over competitors which is achieved by offering the customer greater benefit through a lower price or added value.
Competitive rivalry	are organisations that compete in the same sector (product or service) and for the same potential customers.
Concurrent control	a form of control where problems are solved in real time.
Conglomerate	a large company that consists of multiple business units commonly providing unrelated products or services.

Congruence	factors coming together in an integrated way, for example, environment, values and resources (E–V–R congruence).
Consolidation	a reduction in size or a simplification of the business model. Consolidation may involve merger or acquisition.
Consortia	*see* Joint venture
Core competence	is a complex mix of skills and resources that provide a distinct competitive advantage. They can be successfully applied to multiple areas within the business and are difficult for competitors to imitate.
Corporate governance	country-specific laws and regulations concerning honesty, fiscal openness, independence and legal responsibility.
Corporate-level strategy	is concerned with the growth and development of multiple business units and includes the overseeing of governance procedures, resource management and acquisitions.
Corporate social responsibility (CSR)	is concerned with the standards and manner in which an organisation under takes its moral responsibilities to the wider society. It is the level of corporate citizenship demonstrated above the minimal requirements of governance and law.
Cost leadership	a focus on efficiencies, typically through improved design and economies of scale.
Customer segmentation	a group of consumers categorised, for example, on the basis of demographics, lifestyle and values.

Differentiation	adding value by providing enhanced performance, service, design or image; commonly linked to a higher price.
Dirigiste	an economic model that is founded on state ownership and financial support.
Discounted cash-flow (DCF)	the value of assets or finance over time. Future assets are given a present value based on risk.
Distinctive capability	are the unique resources and competences of an organisation that enable it to achieve competitive advantage.
Diversification	a movement into new markets with new products.
Downstream	functions in a value chain or value network that include distribution, marketing, service and support.
Economies of scale	an increase in scale reduces the cost per unit, typically by reducing manufacturing, marketing and distribution costs.
Economies of scope	increasing the range of products or services reduces the cost per unit, typically by reducing the demand-side costs of marketing and distribution.
Environmental scanning	the process of evaluating the external environment at the macro and micro level in order to identify organisational threats and opportunities.
Exit barrier	describes the difficulty in withdrawing from a market or sector.
Explicit knowledge	knowledge that can be shared, stored and copied.

Exporting
the supply of goods or services to another country or region.

External development
organisational growth by external means, such as franchising, joint ventures or acquisition.

Far environment
see Macro environment

Feasibility of strategy
an assessment of the likely success of the strategy, in particular with regards to the availability of resources, skills and finance.

Federal Trade Commission (FTC)
a government body that regulates competitive practice in the USA.

Feed-back control
a form of control that identifies actions after the event.

Feed-forward control
a form of control that anticipates problems.

First-mover advantage
an early entrant to a market, which enables the setting of market expectations and competitive advantage.

Fixed costs
those costs that do not change in relation to the level of business.

Foreign direct investment (FDI)
a long-term overseas investment where control is maintained by the parent organisation.

Franchising
a form of licensing agreement where the parent company provides the franchisee with a package of resources, including technical help and marketing assistance, in return for a share in the profits.

Globalisation
the process of unification of business, societies and cultures around the world,

resulting in global influence on local activities.

Hierarchy

a series of levels in an organisation where each level is subordinate to a higher level.

Horizontal integration

an organisational alliance, merger or acquisition in the same industry in order to increase market share.

Hybrid strategy

a combination of differentiation with cost leadership or price-based strategies.

Industry

a group of companies that provide similar products or services.

Information and communication technologies (ICT)

computer-based communication systems.

Innovation

the process by which a creative idea is turned into a product or process and which may then be used to generate a competitive advantage.

Intangible resource

non-monetary assets that cannot be easily quantified (e.g. employee skills, partnerships, patents and competences).

Internal development

growth by the use of the organisation's own resources and capabilities when developing products and services.

Joint venture

a strategic alliance or consortium that results in the formation of a new company jointly owned by the parent companies.

Just-in-time (JIT)

an inventory technique which reduces the need for storage of 'in-process' inventory, thereby reducing costs.

Knowledge management

the active management of the intellectual capabilities of an organisation.

Laissez-faire	an economic model based on profit and which broadly encourages free market competition with little political involvement.
Leverage	a term coined by Hamel and Prahalad (1993) relating to the use of specific skills or resources from one part of the organisation to another.
Licensing	a product or service is manufactured or used by another organisation in return for the payment of royalties.
Logical incrementalism	a shorter-term experimental approach to strategic development where strategies tend to be introduced on an unstructured or emergent basis.
Macro environment	far environment characterised by the influences that will affect every firm in the same industry (or sectors) and often other industries, but is unlikely to be influenced by the industry.
Managing shareholder value (MSV)	the combined strategies that are undertaken by a firm to optimise the share price.
Market	is defined by consumer or customer requirements, which in turn may be segmented by demographics, values, behaviours, etc.
Market pull	a reactive development resulting from customer requirements.
Market segment	is defined by consumer or customer requirements and by demographics, values, behaviours, etc.
Merger	is the mutually agreed joining of two similarly sized companies to form a new company. Shares in the new company are distributed to all the previous shareholders.

Micro environment	near environment characterised by the competitive dynamics and markets within the industry or sector. The industry is likely to be able to influence micro environmental factors.
Mission statement	guidelines from which objectives can be set and which in turn will lead to the creation of strategies.
Monopolies and Mergers Commission (MMC)	*see* Competition Commission
Multinational corporation (MNC)	an organisation that owns businesses in more than one country.
Near environment	*see* Micro environment
Non-executive director (NED)	an unpaid executive who is responsible for the governance of the organisation while independently evaluating the strategies and performance of the organisation.
Non-governmental organisation (NGO)	a non-profit-making organisation that commonly supports humanitarian, social, environmental or development issues.
Not-for-profit organisation (NFP)	an organisation that exists solely to support charitable, civil or social purposes.
Off-shoring	the outsourcing of a business process from one country to another, commonly to take advantage of lower costs or to gain access to skills and resources.
Operational strategy	functional strategies to deliver corporate and business strategies with a particular emphasis on quality and efficiency.
Organisational culture	a set of beliefs, behavioural norms and values unconsciously formed by the organisation's workforce.

Organisational knowledge   the product of both learning and experience, it is shared between employees and accumulated through processes and systems.

Outsourcing   subcontracting a process to a third-party organisation, typically to reduce costs or to improve focus on the core business.

Paradigm (cultural)   the summative pattern of beliefs, behaviours, structures and processes.

Planned development   *see* Prescriptive development

Prescriptive development   the long-term planned or rational process of analysing the organisation and the environment in order to determine where the organisation is and where it wants to be. Strategic decisions are commonly made in a sequential and rational manner.

Procedural rationality   choices and decisions made on the basis of tools and theories.

Procurement   purchasing or acquisition of goods or services for the benefit of the organisation.

Product life cycle (PLC)   the stages that a product goes through from design to withdrawal.

Product portfolio   a range of products provided by the same company for different market segments.

Public Private Partnership (PPP)   a business venture between a government and a private organisation. Commonly, the private organisation runs the business on behalf of the government.

Resource-based view (RBV)   a consideration of the resources and capabilities of the organisation and value chain, with a view to exploiting them as a competitive advantage.

Resources

the total means and assets available to an organisation in order for it to survive, including equipment, labour and skills.

Retrenchment

the cutting back or reduction of business activities and expenses in order to focus on the core business.

Return on capital employed (ROCE)

a ratio measure of the returns being achieved from assets or invested capital.

Risk management

the assessment of risk with a view to managing the consequences.

Satisfice

the term coined by Herbert Simon (1955) to describe sub-optimal decision-making and compromise due to previous experience and external and internal pressures.

Small-to-medium enterprise (SME)

an organisation whose head count falls between certain limits. In the EU these are defined as between 50 and 250 employees.

Stakeholders

the individuals and groups that are affected by or impact upon the performance of the organisation.

Strategic alliance

a partnership agreement between two or more companies to form a liaison that aims to reduce risk and achieve a mutually desired outcome.

Strategic analysis

the use of tools to determine the relative strengths and weaknesses of an organisation and the threats and opportunities that may impact upon it from the external environment.

Strategic business unit

the part of an organisation that can be related to a specific range of products or services or market.

Strategic capability   the resources and competences of an organisation that enable it to successfully compete.

Strategic control   corporate control which aims to manage the behaviour, performance and efficiencies of a diverse range of business interests.

Strategic drift   occurs when organisations do not adequately address the long-term strategic position of the organisation in relation to the environment, which results in underperformance.

Strategic group   a group of companies competing in the same industry, for the same customers and with similar strategies.

Strategic management   is the process of identifying, evaluating and implementing strategies in order to meet the organisational objectives.

Stretching   a term coined by Hamel and Prahalad (1993) which refers to the exploitation of existing organisational resources and knowledge.

Suitability of strategy   an evaluation of the proposed strategy to ensure that key organisational issues have been addressed.

Synergy   the added benefit obtained from joining two or more organisations together. The sum of the parts is greater than the individual contributions.

Tacit knowledge   knowledge based on personal experience, it is difficult to communicate and is only developed through practice.

Takeover   *see* Acquisition

Tangible resource	assets that can be quantified, including cash and inventory.
Technology push	the use of emergent scientific developments which benefit customers in a way they have not anticipated.
Threshold resources	the minimal resources required in order to compete in a market.
Total Quality Management (TQM)	the continuous monitoring and incremental improvement of processes within the organisation, with the aim of improving quality and customer satisfaction.
Transnational corporation (TNC)	a multinational firm that gains location benefits and achieves global learning while remaining locally responsive.
Unique resources	resources that are difficult to obtain and provide a clear opportunity for competitive advantage.
Upstream	functions in a value chain or value network that include supply, inbound logistics and operations.
Value chain	the organisational process where value is added to the raw materials (or service) during the process of transformation to the final product (or service). Value chains are typically optimised for efficiency and quality.
Value network	the extended value chain that includes relationships with external partners.
Vertical integration	an alliance, merger or acquisition with an organisation in the supply (backward/upstream) or distribution (forward/downstream) industry.
Virtual organisation	a collaborative network of outsourced functions centrally coordinated using information and communication technologies (ICT).

references

Andrews, K. (1971) *The Concept of Corporate Strategy.* Homewood, IL: R.D. Irwin.

Ansoff, H. (1965) *Corporate Strategy: An Analytical Approach to Business Policy for Growth and Expansion.* New York: McGraw-Hill.

Ansoff, H. (1988) *Corporate Strategy.* London: Penguin.

Argenti, J. (1980) *Practical Corporate Planning.* London: George Allen & Unwin.

Balogun, J. and Hope Hailey, V. (1999) *Exploring Strategic Change.* Harlow: Prentice Hall.

Barney, J.B. (2002) *Gaining and Sustaining Competitive Advantage,* 2nd edn. Upper Saddle River, NJ: Pearson Education.

Belbin, R.M. (1993) *Team Roles at Work.* Oxford: Elsevier Butterworth Heinemann.

Buzan, T. (1993) *The Mind Map Book.* London: BBC.

Buzan, T. (2006) *Speed Reading: Accelerate Your Speed and Understanding for Success.* Harlow: BBC Active.

Chandler, A.D. (1962) *Strategy and Structure: Chapters in the History of the American Industrial Enterprise.* Cambridge, MA: MIT Press.

Contractor, F.J. and Lorange, P. (1988) 'Why should firms cooperate? The strategy and economics basis for cooperative ventures', in F.J. Contractor and P. Lorange, (Eds) *Cooperative Strategies in International Business.* Lexington, MA: D.C. Heath.

Coulter, M. (2008) *Strategic Management in Action,* 4th edn. Upper Saddle River, NJ: Pearson Education.

D'Aveni, R. (1995) *Hypercompetitive Rivalries: Competing in Highly Dynamic Environments.* New York: The Free Press.

Davenport, T.H. and Prusak, L. (1998) *Working Knowledge: How Organizations Manage What they Know.* Boston, MA: Harvard Business School Press.

De Bono, E. (1967) *New Think: The Use of Lateral Thinking in the Generation of New Ideas.* New York: Basic Books.

Faulker, D. and Bowman, C. (1995) *The Essence of Competitive Strategy.* Harlow: Prentice Hall.

Galbraith, J.R. and Kazanjian, R.K. (1986) *Strategy Implementation,* 2nd edn. St Paul, MN: West Publishing.

Goleman, D. (1995) *Emotional Intelligence: Why it Can Matter Move than IQ.* New York: Bantam Books.

Hamel, G, and Prahalad, C.K. (1990) 'The core competence of the corporation', *Harvard Business Review* 68(3): 79–91.

Hamel, G. and Prahalad, C.K. (1993) 'Strategy as stretch and leverage', *Harvard Business Review* 71: 75–84, March–April.

Handy, C. (1993) *Understanding Organisations,* 4th edn. Harmondsworth: Penguin.

Johnson, G., (1992) 'Managing strategic change: strategy culture and action', *Long Range Planning* 25(1): 28–36.

Johnson, G. Scholes, K. and Whittington, R. (2008) *Exploring Corporate Strategy,* 8th edn. Harlow: Pearson Education.

Kolb, D.A. (1984) *Experiential Learning.* Englewood Cliffs, NJ: Prentice-Hall.

Lewin, K. (1952) *Field Theory in Social Science.* London: Tavistock.

Lindblom, C.E. (1959) 'The science of muddling through', *Public Administration Review* 19: 79–88.

Lynch, R. (2006) *Corporate Strategy,* 4th edn. Harlow: Pearson Education.

Mendelow, A. (1991) Stakeholders and strategic human resource development. *Proceedings of the Second International Conference on Information Systems.* Cambridge, MA.

Miles, R.E. and Snow, C.C. (1978) *Organizational Strategy, Structure, and Process.* New York: McGraw-Hill.

Mintzberg, H. (1990) 'The design school: reconsidering the basic premise of strategic management', *Strategic Management Journal* 11: 171–95.

Mintzberg, H. and Quinn, J.B (1992) *The Strategy Process.* Englewood Cliffs, NJ: Prentice Hall.

Nonaka, I. and Takeuchi, H. (1995) *The Knowledge Creating Company.* Oxford: Oxford University Press.

Porter, M.E. (1980) *Competitive Strategy: Techniques for Analysing Industries and Competitors.* New York: The Free Press.

Porter, M.E. (1985) *Competitive Advantage: Creating and Sustaining Competitive Performance.* New York: The Free Press.

Porter, M.E. (1990) *The Competitive Advantage of Nations.* New York: The Free Press.

Porter, M.E. (2008) 'The five competitive forces that shape strategy', *Harvard Business Review* 86: 78–93, January.

Quinn. J.B. (1980) *Strategies for Change: Logical Incrementalism.* Homewood, IL: Irwin.

Simon, H.A. (1955) 'A behavioural model of rational choice', *Quarterly Journal of Economics* 69: 99–118.

Simon, H.A. (1960) *The New Science of Management Decision.* Englewood Cliffs, NJ: Prentice Hall.

Simon, H. (1974) 'How big is a chunk?', *Science* 183: 482–88.

Thompson, J.L. and Martin, F. (2005) *Strategic Management: Awareness, Analysis and Change,* 5th edn. London: Thompson Learning.

Whittington, R., Pettigrew, A., Peck, S., Fenton, E. and Conyon, M. (1999) 'Change and complementarities in the new competitive landscape', *Organisational Science* 10(5): 583–600.

Yip, G. (2003) *Total Global Strategy.* Harlow: FT/Prentice Hall.

author index

Bold = key page
Italic = glossary entry

subject index

Bold = key page
Italic = glossary entry